COWGIRLS

WOMEN OF THE WILD WEST

Sydney Gamble - Photo

DEDICATION

For my grandmother, Betty Flood,
whose pluck and youth have always
been an inspiration.

Copyright © 2000
ZON INTERNATIONAL PUBLISHING COMPANY

Published by Zon International Publishing Company
P.O.Box 6459, Santa Fe, New Mexico 87502, U.S.A.
Telephone: 505/ 995-0102; Fax: 505/ 995-0103

ISBN 0-939549-18-2

First Edition

Printed in Singapore

Library of Congress Cataloging-in-Publication Data
Flood, Elizabeth Clair, 1967-
    Cowgirls : Women of the Wild West / by
Elizabeth Clair Flood & William Manns ; foreword by
Dale Evans. – 1st ed.
        p.   cm.
    Includes bibliographical references and index.
    ISBN 0-939549-18-2
    1. Cowgirls–West (U.S.)–History Pictorial works.
2. ranch life–West (U.S.)–History Pictorial works. 3.
West (U.S.)–Social life and customs Pictorial works.
I. Manns, William. II. Title.

F596.F568 1999
978'.03'0922–dc21
99-28756 CIP

COWGIRLS

WOMEN OF THE WILD WEST

ELIZABETH CLAIR FLOOD

PHOTOGRAPHY BY WILLIAM MANNS

FOREWORD BY DALE EVANS

EDITED BY HELENE SAGE

ZON INTERNATIONAL PUBLISHING COMPANY
SANTA FE • NEW MEXICO

ACKNOWLEDGMENTS

This project spun out of the chute with the generous help of many collectors, experts, and institutions. We are deeply indebted to the following individuals who shared their cowgirl collections: Rick Bachman, Jim and Rita Boniello, Cindy DeBeer, Wild Bill Cleaver, Douglas Deihl, Elmer Diederich, Jimmy Filler, Dawn Fisher, Mort and Donna Fleischer, Joe Gish, William Healey, Francine Hengesbaugh, Douglas Harman, Pris Hodges, Jim Holley, Matt Johnson, Bob Hunn, George Jackson, Don King, Linda Kohn, Brian Lebel, Jack Long, Al Luevand, Bill Mackin, Fred Miller, Ruth and Jerry Murphey, Robert and Steph Murphy, Jim Naramore, Danny Neill, Bob Nelson, Mary Nyhom, Jill O'Connor, Dan Pauly, George Pittman, John and Peggy Pokrifcsak, Larry Robertson, Helene Sage, Steve Sheppard, Joseph Sherwood, Lester Silva, Jack Slaughter, Charlie Smith, Ron Soodalter, Phil and Linda Spangenberger, Nancy Walden, Wyle Walden, Todd Wideman, and Jim Williams.

We owe a special debt of gratitude to Barbara Schmitt and Mary Schmitt of Cayuse Western Americana. Both shared their exquisite cowgirl collection and answered our never-ending questions.

Special thanks to Judy Benson and to Lindsey and Nancy Enderby for their encouragement and interest in this project.

Of course, the support of Dale Evans, the Queen of the West, and of her children Cheryl and Dusty Rogers, was an unexpected bonus. We are grateful for their enthusiasm.

Others along the trail inspired us. Our deepest thanks to those western women who shared their stories: Nancy Bragg-Witmar, Polly Burson, Dorothy Dellagana, DeDe Merritt, Dixie Mosely, Alice Renner, Mitzi Lucas Riley, Sammy Thurman, Alice Van-Springsteen, and the Rodeo Grandmas Janis Capezzoli Anderson, Peggy Minor Hunt, Lorraine Plass, Judy Golladay, and Chloe Weidenbach. A special thanks to Corinne Williams whose brilliant stories and constant flow of colorful letters cheered me on.

Important people and organizations who supported us include: Lynn Arambel, Bruce and Julianne Bartlett, Matt Bishop, Tona Blake, Kate Cabbott, Chuck Cooper, Daryl Cozad, Tuda and Jack Crews, Henley Farnes, Margaret Formby, Max Golladay, Kurt House, Jerry Jaz, Bill Lawrence, Gini Lawson, Doris Loeser, Jack Long, Teddi and Milo Marks, Molly Morrow, Ramona and John Niland, Emmy Lou Precott, C.J. Reynolds, Pat Riley, Danielle Routhier, Drew and Bear Simmons, Washington Mutual, Jim Walker of McCann-Erickson in Seattle, Dale Windham, Gail Woerner, and Ed Wren.

We were delighted for access to unusual historic photos from the private collections of: Kathy Bressler, Jim Cantwell, Wild Bill Cleaver, Fighting Bear Antiques, Douglas Harman, Polly Helm, Matt Johnson, Wayne Low, Robert Manns, Marilee Montana, Robert and Steph Murphy, Mike and Joy Painter, Herb Peck, Buck Rainey, Richard Rattenbury, Norina Shields, Jack Slaughter, and Marsha Wallgren.

The following museums and institutions provided invaluable research material, old documents, and historic photographs, and in many cases allowed us to photograph their important artifacts. Thank-you to Amon Carter Museum, Arizona Historical Society, Austin Public Library, Autry Museum of Western Heritage, Belden Museum, Buffalo Bill Historical Center, Buffalo Bill Memorial Museum, Circus World Museum, C.M. Russell Museum, Colorado Historical Society, Denver Public Library Western History Department, Glenbow Archives, Houston Stock Show and Rodeo, Montana Historical Society, Monterey County Historical Society, National Cowboy Hall of Fame, National Cowgirl Museum and Hall of Fame, New Mexico State Archives, Museum of Northwestern Colorado, Old West Museum, Oregon Historical Society, Prairie County Historical Society, Teton County Historical Society, University of Oklahoma Western History Collection, University of Wyoming American Heritage Center, and Wyoming State Archives.

One last thank-you to our editor Helene Sage, who provided invaluable wisdom and support.

CONTENTS

FOREWORD

BY DALE EVANS

I never felt the cowgirl received enough attention. It was always the cowboy. Outside of Calamity Jane and Annie Oakley, there were very few cowgirls people knew about. I was never a real cowgirl, but because I was from Texas, the role was a natural. I shared the cowgirl's streak of independence and gusto for life.

When I was a child I loved Texas with a passion. I was born in Uvalde, just about ninety miles southwest of San Antonio. When I was six we moved to Arkansas, but we used to go back to my aunt Annie and uncle Byron's ranch in Uvalde where I swam the Nueces river and rode a goat or a pony or anything I could get on. All of Texas seemed like a grand romance in those days - so wild and free. And I was nutty about cowboys. I used to say that when I grew up I was going to marry Tom Mix. I was quite certain he would wait for me and that he would never change. While galloping our horses through sagebrush, we would have six children and the world would be as sweet as it could be.

And then there came a time after I was twelve or thirteen years old that I thought I was a little too sophisticated for cowboys or riding, so I pursued a career singing on the radio and at supper clubs. One of my first big breaks was in Chicago in 1939 when I was hired by CBS for station WBBN. I was twenty-six years old. They called my show "That Gal From Texas." I sang songs like "Under The Texas Moon" and "My Heart is Down Texas Way."

Out of the blue I received a telegram from Hollywood to come out for a screen test. And after doing six pictures in Hollywood, Republic paired Roy Rogers and me in a film called *The Cowboy and the Señorita*. This was in 1944. By this time

Roy was rapidly climbing in popularity. He was almost number one. But, there was one difficulty for me: Republic Studios never asked if I could ride a horse. They just assumed I could since I was from Texas. But I was awful on horseback. That's what happens when you ride goats instead of horses. When Roy first saw me in the saddle he said he'd never seen so much sky between a woman and a horse in his life.

Naturally, I decided to take riding lessons at Pickwick Stables in North Hollywood. I needed the lessons if I was going to perform on Buttermilk, that buckskin quarter horse with his beautiful black mane and tail. Buttermilk was sweet, but had an awful gait, and he changed leads if he hit a curb. Buttermilk could run like the wind and could take Trigger in the short distances. Roy used to get so mad; he used to yell, "Pull him up! Pull him up! Pull him up!," because he didn't ever want him ahead of Trigger. But Trigger was the greatest horse I'd ever seen in my life. The minute he got his stride he passed everything; he'd leave Buttermilk like he was standing still.

Early on, I wasn't a very attentive horsewoman. One day when Roy and I were filming our third or fourth movie together, I was in high-heel shoes with my leg slung over the saddle horn. I was sitting listening to Gabby Hayes practicing some dialogue, laughing at the way he twisted that wrinkled old face of his when he spit out his words. At one point I laughed so hard that I threw my head back and slapped my side. The horse took my sudden reaction as a signal to bolt - and bolt he did, like he was shot from a cannon! I had no grip or anything, but Roy chased us and plucked me off the saddle, pulling me up close to him on Trigger's back.

In most of my movies, I played a smart aleck. I wasn't the sweet little lady, waiting to be saved. I was independent, both on and off the screen. I liked to do things my way. In *My Pal Trigger* (my favorite of all the pictures Roy and I did together), I decided against a stunt woman. I wanted to ride.

In this film I had to run a race on an English saddle. I had never ridden English before but I was going to do it if it killed me. So when it was time to shoot the scene, I walked up to the director and said, "I'm riding, and I don't want a double. I'm doing it." He replied, "No you're not," but I got up there on that Thoroughbred with those little short stirrups with nothing to hold onto, no saddle horn, no nothing except a scroungy old mane, and he took off wide open. It had rained, so there was mud coming up in my face from the camera truck; I couldn't see a thing. Later while I was mopping the muck from my face, the

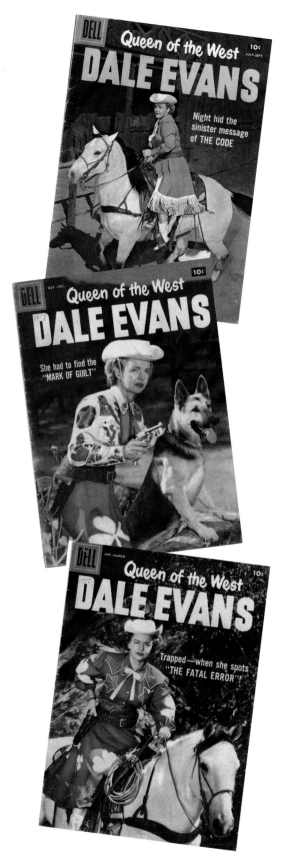

A series of twenty-three Dale Evans comic books was published by Dell Comics from 1953 to 1959. Evans portrayed a hard-riding crack shot in her TV show and in these comics. AC Comics Collection.

producer, Mandy Schaffer, scolded me, "Dale, that's the silliest thing you'll ever do in your life. You could have fallen off that horse; you could have cost the studio thousands upon thousands of dollars. I feel like taking you across my knee and spanking you. Don't you ever, as long as you work in a picture with me, ever do that again."

I said, "But, I stayed on, didn't I?" Although when I finally saw *My Pal Trigger*, I couldn't tell it was me riding the horse at all.

When I first met Roy, I thought he was quite good looking, but rather shy. At Republic we were teamed up regularly. In the fall of 1947, at the rodeo in Chicago, we were on our horses, in the chutes, waiting to be introduced, when Roy said, "Dale, what are you doing New Year's Eve?"

New Year's Eve was still months away. I had no plans.

Then he reached into his pocket and pulled out a small box. Inside it was a gold ring set with rubies. He reached down for my hand and slipped the ring on my finger. "Well then," he said. "Why don't we get married?"

The drum roll sounded, the lights dimmed, Trigger reared up, and Roy Rogers galloped into the arena to the thunder of applause. I followed, on cue, and our horses took their position side by side in the spotlight in front of thousands of people. Before lifting the microphone to sing the National Anthem, I turned to look at Roy. He looked back at me, beaming with delight. The din of cheers made it impossible to speak. I formed the word 'Yes' with my lips. He nodded, and we began to sing.

When we married, the studio took me out of Roy's pictures. I wasn't real happy about that, but I had my hands full with three of Roy's children (whose mother had died), one of my own, and our new baby, Robin, who had Downs syndrome.

Just days after we brought Robin home from the hospital, I got to thinking about the music on "The Roy Rogers Show" on the radio. Roy had a cute theme song at the time called "Smiles are Made Out of the Sunshine." It was popular, but I felt it wasn't western enough, and it didn't say enough about what it means to be a cowboy - especially when, as Roy and I had learned, the trails you ride aren't always sunny ones. Roy had the habit of autographing his publicity photos with "Many Happy Trails" or "Trails of Happiness" and I thought, that's what he needs - a trail song. I remembered a story my mother had told me about the guides hollering to each other in the Grand Canyon, and I was inspired by the music of

"The Grand Canyon Suite." I wrote "Happy Trails" in three hours, then I went down to the radio station and taught it to all the boys. I also wrote "Don't Ever Fall In Love with a Cowboy ('Cause He'll Love His Horse the Best)," as a gag because Trigger always got top billing over me.

After Robin was born, I made three films, then Roy and I got into television, and I began writing books, one of which was *Angel Unawares*, a best seller about Robin, who died when she was two years old.

One afternoon in my own living room, the boys (Dusty and Sandy) were wrestling and rolling all over the floor and knocking things over. I was tired of hearing myself repeating: "Stop it. Stop it. You're going to knock something over that will set the house on fire" - but they just ignored me. So, I ran all the way down the hall toward the big closet where I kept my show pistol and gun belt, and grabbed a whole bunch of blanks, loaded my gun, and ran back in there shooting blanks off just as fast as I could. "Sorry boys," I said. "But I needed to get your attention." In those years, my family kept me busy, as did our businesses. I had a full plate.

Throughout my life, I always hoped children would be inspired by the courage and independence of the characters Roy and I played. When we visited orphanages, we found many children who aspired to be cowboys or cowgirls. For me, the spirit of the cowgirl was contagious. The cowgirl's independent character suited me. I was, after all, Texan.

I'm happy the cowgirl is finally getting her due in this comprehensive book by Elizabeth Clair Flood and William Manns, for she deserves all the attention she can get. What I always hoped that children learned from the cowgirls I played was bravery and confidence. I hope the cowgirl and her image continues to inspire these values in all of us.

Dale Evans Rogers

Dale Evans was born Frances Octavia Smith, October 31, 1912 in Uvalde, Texas. She pursued a career in music that included singing in nightclubs, on the radio, and with a variety of bands in Tennessee. In 1939, under her show name Dale Evans, she worked for WBBM, the CBS station in Chicago. Talent scouts soon discovered her and arranged for a screen test in Hollywood for the movie Holiday Inn, starring Fred Astaire and Bing Crosby. Several years and several films later, Republic Studios cast their leading star Roy Rogers with Dale Evans in The Cowboy and the Señorita (1944), the first of twenty-eight films they would do together. Dale Evans married Roy Rogers on New Year's Eve, 1947. In 1950, Roy and Dale developed their own company and began producing their popular half-hour television series, "The Roy Rogers Show," that ran until 1957. Rogers died in 1998. Evans still lives in Victorville, California near The Roy Rogers-Dale Evans Museum. She continues to write books, star in a weekly television show called "A Date With Dale," and enjoy sixteen grandchildren and over thirty great-grandchildren.

INTRODUCTION

Two years ago, I sat on a curb in front of an Albertson's grocery store in Banning, California, waiting for Corinne Williams. Mitzi Riley, daughter of the famous 1920s rodeo cowgirl, Tad Lucas, and a successful trick-rider in her own right, told me Williams could help me understand the cowgirl character. Having lived in Wyoming for nearly nine years, I had some idea about the definition of a cowgirl. Like the cowboy, I associated the cowgirl with cows, ranch life, and rodeo. I believed her to be independent, spirited, and a good hand with horses. Because I've watched old movies, with stars like Barbara Stanwyck and Dale Evans, I also couldn't help believing that cowgirls wore gingham shirts and Stetsons, spoke sweetly, and looked glamorous all the time.

Suddenly, a rattletrap Chevy pickup pulled up in front of me and a blond woman in an old cap, with pigtails tied in rawhide, waved and hollered at me. She leapt from her truck to shake my hand and introduced herself as Corinne Williams. Standing five feet, ten inches tall, somewhere in her late sixties, Williams suggested that we grab some fried chicken and coleslaw and head back to the ranch where she worked.

In her camping trailer, Williams told me she'd grown up with "finger bowls and protocol" in New Jersey under the supervision of her grandmother. "She taught me to ride English and sing," Williams said. "She judged people by their diction and their handwriting. She wanted me to grow up to be a lady." When Williams found herself in a foster home at the age of nine, in and out of boarding schools, she developed her own ideas about what she wanted from life.

"When I was a child, I wanted adventure. I grew up watching Roy Rogers and Gene Autry. I dreamed of adventures like the ones they had," she said. Seeking excitement, Williams ran away from her foster families on a number of occasions to look for cowgirl work. At sixteen she landed her first cowgirl job, as a hand on the 76 ranch in Arizona. Since most of the young cowboys were occupied in some capacity with World War II, a bunk house full of reluctant, grumpy old cowboys taught Williams to feed, fix fence, and shoe horses. One summer she bulldogged steers with the cowboys and sang during ropings. Never able to stay in one place, Williams drifted from ranch work to odd jobs, including a short stint racking pool in Blackfoot, Idaho where she played snooker with the Indians.

In 1949, after loading a truck of hay for the Wrangler Association in Sedona, Arizona, in hopes of securing a job with them on the movie set of *Broken Arrow*, the Association refused to hire Williams full-time because she was a woman. Soon thereafter, cowgirls Tad Lucas and Lucyle Richards, who were both rodeo stars in the 1920s and 1930s, encouraged Williams to move to Fort Worth, Texas and learn to rodeo. From the cowboy entrepreneur Texas Kid, Jr. she learned how to "lurch" broncs out of a shotgun chute (an early chute from which three sides fell to the ground, for the rider and horse to jump clear). Thus, bulldogging and riding broncs in the daytime, singing and playing the guitar in the evening, Williams drifted among rodeos and Wild West shows.

"When you ain't got nobody anywhere but a dog you get restless," she said. "All I had was a duffel bag, a footlocker, and a guitar. All I thought about was wild horses and how I wanted to be a good hand."

Photographs of Williams's life as a bulldogger, a rodeo performer who jumps from horseback to wrestle a steer to the ground, papered the walls of her trailer. She wore satin pants and roses in her hair: "I tried to look pretty. You're not going to sell if you look tough." In one year she bulldogged ninety-two steers.

From 1959 to 1966, Williams was a popular contract act in many of the western states and was known as the world's only lady bulldogger during this time. She also participated in bronc riding, trick-riding, and trick-roping events. The rodeo world welcomed her and for the first time she felt that she had a supportive family. "In the rodeo world, you help a guy put his foot in the stirrup, he helps you," she said.

In the early sixties, Williams met President Truman at a rodeo in Independence, Missouri. After watching Williams wrestle an ornery steer to the ground and rock on the hurricane deck of a bucking bronc, Truman approached her on the announcer's stage and winked. "Couldn't you find an easier way to make a living?" he asked. Williams laughed. She was making $100 *per* bronc and $100 for bulldogging, a lot of money in those days, and had two children to support. Most importantly, she liked the adventure of her gypsy lifestyle.

"This is a hard life and you get hard with it," Williams told me, as she pulled out her electric piano and prepared to play a song. "It's not the PTA. And it's not about how you put on your earrings."

I liked this itinerant woman. She had spunk, courage, originality, and optimism despite the difficulties she had experienced. She raised two children on the road, often without an adequate income, and now hobbles around on a titanium ankle and knee (results of life in the arena). Williams jokes with no regrets about

11

her being a tin woodman with no oil. After singing "Morning has Broken" from her trailer porch, Williams asked me if I'd like to see her trick-rope. "Of course!"

From somewhere inside her trailer she pulled out an old, round tin. Standing a little crookedly on her metal ankle, she slowly extricated the rope and, with a smile full of confidence, sent the rope sailing into the air and into one enormous loop which spun around her head. The joy of that moment, and especially Williams's sense of personal value, made me want to rediscover the American cowgirl, whose spirit seemed to thrive on adventure and an unconventional life on the fringes of civilization. Her self-confidence and her beauty — her originality — seemed to grow directly out of the frontier. As I assembled notes from museum archives, sifted through the extensive files at the National Cowgirl Museum and Hall of Fame in Fort Worth, read many autobiographies and memoirs of pioneer women, and tracked down old cowgirls from California to Texas, I uncovered countless inspiring tales about the joys and hardships of frontier women. Although every woman was clearly unique, they all shared a hardy, youthful spirit, and a gusto for life which I both admired and envied.

Whereas women like Williams actively chose to be cowgirls, there were and still are many born into the role. In the 1880s, women like Cattle Kate and Evelyn Cameron made conscious decisions to abandon a restrictive Victorian environment in hopes of finding a more fulfilling life in the West. These women, who encountered an unfenced land, were followed by young girls who grew up on Western ranches at the turn of the century, cowgirls because of their environment. Families had modest incomes and ranch work required many hands. Boys and girls were put to work feeding, chasing wild horses, and herding cattle across the sagebrush. Young girls learned from their accomplishments that they were as capable as their brothers. Competing in Wild West shows and rodeoing were viable ways to make a living out West for both sexes. Many of the women I met, however, shrugged off my lavish praise for their nerve and prowess in competition against men: "It was just a job."

In the 1920s, the cowgirl charmed audiences around the world with her talent and style. For the most part, cowgirls worked and competed alongside cowboys. Largely unaware of women flaunting their independence in New York speakeasies or Parisian night clubs, cowgirls cast off corsets and sidesaddles in practicality rather than rebellion. Many of the cowgirls preferred working cattle to campaigning for the vote, and riding broncs to discussing women's new-found independence. A reporter from the *Gazette* in St. Joseph, Missouri wrote in 1909: "Miss Mulhall is

Tad Lucas, rodeo cowgirl, 1925.

too busy roping steers, riding wild horses, and entertaining the public to give the suffragette movement much thought."

Wild West shows in the 1880s presented the cowgirl as a beautiful, daring woman. Inspired by an exciting life on the road, some of these performers, for example, Lucille Mulhall, grew up on ranches, but others, like the Norwegian hairdresser Tillie Baldwin, ran away from home. At the turn of the century, dime novels and postcards publicized the beauty of these bold women, who were often portrayed wearing large hats and galloping across the plains. Hollywood later appropriated and, in some cases, exploited the image. For the most part the cowgirl was portrayed as a feminine ranch girl who had spunk but looked best in the company of her man. Many of the real cowgirls disapproved of this Hollywood image, but unquestionably both movies and television helped to propel the cowgirl into the urban American home.

As early as the 1880s, Eastern sophisticates traveled West to spend time on ranches. Riding, roping, or dining, these women dressed the part in big hats, fancy boots, and Indian-beaded vests. Foregoing tennis and debutante parties, they galloped across open country and enjoyed a taste of the adventure and independence that had once belonged to the old-time cowgirl.

From the beginning, the cowgirl received worldwide attention for her sense of style. Her attitude toward clothing revealed much about her character, layered as it was with contradictions and surprises. She was practical; she was professional; she was feminine, and in many cases as capable, daring, and/or irresponsible as any cowboy. In *Cowgirls*, photographs of old clothes and cowgirl gear illustrate the evolution of the cowgirl from the Victorian women who discarded their petticoats, to the rodeo girls who wore sequins and satin, to the women ranchers and professional athletes who now wear blue jeans. Some of the most exotic costumes were worn in the Wild West shows and in rodeos between 1910-1930. The Wyoming cowgirl Prairie Rose Henderson captured the attention of audiences worldwide, with her engaging smile, broad-brimmed hat, and eccentric, usually homemade outfit: a blouse trimmed in chiffon and sequins, and a wide band of marabou feathers hanging over bloomers, stockings, and cowboy boots.

Throughout this project I struggled to find information proving that the cowgirl was not simply a myth fabricated by Wild West shows, Hollywood, and television, or another cliché for American independence. I was delighted to discover an original character who, like the cowboy, was motivated by a passion for challenge and the need to make a living. She worked with cattle on ranches or excelled in the arenas of Wild West shows and rodeos, often side-by-side with the cowboy. Many a woman accentuated the romance that immediately enveloped her character with outfits sporting fringed skirts, inlaid boots, and colorful ribbons. The old-time cowgirl glowed with all the feminine pluck and impudence of Colette, mixed with a strength of character, all of which took root and blossomed in the western United States over the years spanning the emergence of the twentieth century. And I discovered that the cowgirl spirit was not only inspiring, but was as unpredictable as Wyoming weather.

Elizabeth Clair Flood
Wilson, Wyoming

RANCH WOMEN

CHAPTER 1

The first cowgirls broke the rules. In the nineteenth century, a woman's place was in the home, not out on the range herding cattle, branding calves, or breaking horses: Victorian society considered this behavior unladylike. Complete with corset, a lady behaved decorously, served tea in the parlor, sewed, and cared for her husband and family. Living on the fringes of society to run a cattle ranch was a preposterous vocation for a woman and represented uncharted territory. Aware of the risks, but determined to succeed, one of Wyoming's first cowgirls was hanged for trying.

In 1889, a group of cattle barons, threatened by the potential success of their neighbors, cattle ranchers Ellen Watson and her husband Jim Averill, hanged them from a pine tree. Just two years before this incident, Watson, dressed in her usual green riding habit, rode sidesaddle from her ranch in Sweetwater County, Wyoming to meet an emigrant on the Oregon Trail, where she purchased his small herd for one dollar a head. Later she seared her herd of sixty-one head with her registered brand, LU (a phonetic symbol of her nickname "Ella"). At this time, Watson was one of the few women in the country who owned her own cows, in addition to a homestead with cabin, corrals, and a sixty-acre pasture fenced with three-wire, four-barbed "bob wire," stapled to sturdy, new cedar posts. Although Watson's husband, who lived on the homestead next door, helped her occasionally, he cared little for the livestock, as he was busy running the post office and a small grocery store. The cows were Watson's responsibility. She must have believed ranching would be more profitable than her past occupations as a cook and domestic.

Watson never succeeded. The murderers, a group of five powerful ranchmen, falsely accused her of trading sexual favors for mavericks. How else could a women possibly obtain so many cows? These men were so influential that they convinced the Wyoming newspapers to print their fabricated story

A hand-tinted portrait of a ranch girl, c. 1910, shows her fancy headstall and silver-mounted spurs. Cleaver Collection.

(opposite) A stylized image of a cowgirl at the turn of the century, used to advertise H. Simkowitz Wearing Apparel, portrays the cowgirl as a wholesome, free-spirited woman.

A cowgirl's possessions of the 1880s were few. She cherished her personal items and often kept them in a small trunk. Diederich Collection.

Ellen Watson and her husband were hanged for cattle rustling in 1889. Watson was thought to have traded sex for stolen cows, but was in actuality dispatched because of her threat to major Wyoming cattle interests. Wyoming State Archives.

justifying their brutal and unforgivable act. Reporter Edward Towse of the *Cheyenne Daily Leader* perpetuated the myth with embellished details and gave the victim the catchy and enduring name, Cattle Kate.

The story of Cattle Kate, the woman rustler and virago who traded sex for cows, has persisted until recently. After years of research, Wyoming historian George Hufsmith uncovered enough information to prove that Ellen Watson and her husband were hard-working pioneers and not cattle thieves. Unfortunately, a handful of wealthy ranchers believed murdering two homesteaders might stop the overwhelming influx of other newcomers ("nesters"), whose smaller ranches infringed on their grazing land. Legend persists that a man named McClain, as he draped the noose around Watson's neck and contended with her writhing and screaming, retorted: "You have to die sometime and one time is as good as another."

Prior to the 1880s, there were few women in the West. Those who traveled there went for different reasons. Like the men who were intrigued by the opportunities and promise of a better life, many women were escaping a soured marriage or a miserable past. Some went simply for adventure. When Wyoming pioneer Mrs. John Cassin Dyer was sixteen, she left her hometown in Iowa for Rawlins, Wyoming in 1873 to live with her sister's family, despite her mother's fears that she would be scalped by Indians. Dyer wrote in her autobiography: "I left with all a girl's enthusiasm for new scenes, filled with what I had pictured as a wonderful adventure, the envy of all my girl friends you may be sure."

Women usually took jobs as cooks, teachers, laundresses, and prostitutes, and occasionally as physicians and lawyers. Looking for trouble, a number of women, like Calamity Jane, roamed the countryside. Pearl Hart and Belle Starr became outlaws. Others trailed reluctantly behind their husbands, sad to leave friends, family, and their civilized communities. These women would soon experience the rigors of housekeeping in a lonely country with few supplies. "Persons afraid of coyotes and work and loneliness had better let ranching alone," said Elinore Stewart, who married a Scottish rancher and commenced her life on a Wyoming ranch in the late 1800s.

Clearly, being a cowgirl was uncommon in the late 1800s, and some women, who longed for a western adventure, masqueraded as cowboys to escape hassle or hanging. It was not only easier but a preferable alternative.

One afternoon in 1888, trail driver Samuel Dunn Houston of San Antonio, Texas hired a few men in Clayton, New Mexico for a spring drive to Colorado. He found "a kid of a boy" at the livery stable who wanted to go up the trail.

In the late 1800s, women accompanied their husbands on round-ups and cattle drives. Many, like the woman second from the left, crossed the Great Plains riding sidesaddle.

Named Willie Matthews, he was nineteen years old, weighed one hundred and twenty-five pounds, and was from Caldwell, Kansas. Houston soon discovered that he was also a good hand. In *The Trail Drivers of Texas* Houston reported:

"The kid would get up the darkest stormy nights and stay with the cattle until the storm was over. He was good natured, very modest, didn't use any cuss words or tobacco, and was always pleasant. . . I was so pleased with him that I wished many times that I could find two or three more like him."

Houston wrote that the drive went smoothly until they reached Hugo, Colorado when Matthews approached him after dinner on the trail and asked if he could quit. "He insisted, said he was homesick, and I had to let him go."

About sundown, all the cowboys were sitting around the campfire when a young lady "all dressed up" approached from the direction of town. Houston was baffled as to why a woman would visit his camp. When the lady was twenty feet from him, she laughed. "Mr. Houston, you don't know me, do you?"

Houston's mouth dropped open. "Kid, is it possible that you are a lady?" He and the rest of his men were dumbfounded. All Houston could think of was what was said on the trail over the last three weeks. He ordered her to sit down on a tomato box and explain herself. She told Mr. Houston that her father was an old-time trail driver from Caldwell. When she was ten or twelve years old,

Texas Cattle Queen Lizzy (Johnson) Williams proved that women, given the same opportunities as men, could build a financial empire from modest investments in the cattle business. When not driving her cattle up the Chisholm Trail, she wore luxurious silks, taffeta, and velvets and owned diamond and emerald jewelry valued then at about $10,000. Austin Public Library.

Because ranch help was limited and men were often out on trail drives, women, dressed in full-length skirts, were expected to help out on the ranch. Two Becker sisters hold a cow in place while a third lady does the branding on Fritz Becker's ranch in San Luis Valley, Colorado in 1894. Denver Public Library, Western History.

Ranch women of the late 1880s, who deigned to wear skirts during the branding and herding of cattle, were frowned upon. Fashions soon changed because women found long skirts imprac- tical and dan- gerous for out- door work. Diederich Collection.

she used to listen to his stories about the cow trails in the 1870s. Fascinated, she vowed that she too would drive cattle one day.

"Now, Mr. Houston, I am glad I found you to make the trip with, for I have enjoyed it," she said as she left for home.

Another woman, Jo Monaghan, departed for the West in men's clothing. Expelled from her family for marrying below her class, and subsequently deserted by her rogue husband, this young debutante traveled West, encouraged by the promise of a better life. She chose to dress like a man to avoid attention while traveling alone or working at men's jobs. After a variety of occupations such as gold miner, sheep herder, and stable hand, she settled into bronco busting and cow punching. After years of hard work, Monaghan purchased a cow, a horse, and some hens and proved-up on a homestead in Rockville, Idaho. She soon increased her herd to several hundred head and added fifty buckskin horses branded "J.O." Only after her death did her neighbors and friends discover that Jo Monaghan was a woman.

Elsa Jane Guerin called herself Charlie Parker and drove a stagecoach along the California coast. She was known throughout the state. "I buried my sex in my heart and roughened the surface so the grave would not be discovered. . .," she said. When Guerin was shot in the belly, as a result of an argument, her friends were shocked to discover that she was a woman.

A number of women pursued western careers with little resistance. Around the time Cattle Kate was hanged, Lizzy (Johnson) Williams proceeded up the Chisholm Trail with a herd of cattle. Like Ellen Watson, Williams was unwilling to sit on the fence and watch men make money on cows. Born in Jefferson City, Missouri in 1843, Lizzy Johnson was the second of six children. At sixteen she taught at her father's school in the Texas countryside and in 1873 she moved to Austin to teach. Intrigued with the opportunity of the cattle

18

Victorian riding gauntlets featuring embroidered roses were often sold at western trading posts. Inspired by cavalry gauntlets, cowboys and cowgirls adopted the style of the work glove embellished with various Indian designs. Lebel Collection.

This stylish turn-of-the-century westerner is wearing a traditional cowgirl outfit: a typical pair of Victorian gauntlets, a short skirt, tall lace-up boots, and a red scarf. Her sash was probably a style adopted from Charlie Russell who, inspired by the vaquero costume, always wore a red sash. Diederich Collection.

(below) Ladies' riding gauntlets came in a wide variety of commercial designs. Many were embroidered with horse shoes and whips, whereas others were decorated in buckskin fringe. Westerners wore gauntlets for work and in the show arena. High Noon Collection.

Broad-brimmed hats were not only a stylish accessory to a cowgirl's outfit, but they also served to protect her face from the blazing sun. A hitched horse-hair hatband decorates this flat crown, six-inch brim hat. Holley Collection.

This cowgirl, wearing a wide-brimmed hat, glows with the independence of a Westerner. The hand-tinted image, published by Schlesinger Brothers of New York, is copyrighted 1912.

Cowgirl hats had regional distinctions. This crown was known as a Montana peak and enjoyed popularity through-out the mid-1880s. Soodalter Collection.

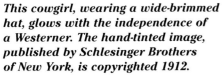

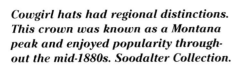

This early cowgirl is outfitted with a six-shooter and a fine sombrero. Hats have always been important in the West, not only for protection from the elements, but as a badge of office that distinguished the cowboy and cowgirl from others on the range.

business, she kept books for the cattlemen in the nearby town of Lockhart, the gathering place for cattle driven up from the brush country of south Texas.

During this time, Johnson wrote stories, e.g., *The Secret Sister*, *The Haunted House Among the Mountains*, and *Lady Inez* or *The Passion Flower, An American Romance*, for popular magazines. Income from this work helped her to underwrite her first cattle investment. In three years, her $2,500 stock in a Chicago cattle company realized a one-hundred percent profit. Johnson subsequently began buying both land and cattle, and in 1871 in Travis County recorded her CY brand that was purchased with a herd of cattle.

When Johnson was thirty-six she married Hezekiah G. Williams. Although it appears that she loved her husband, she was unimpressed with his business skills and was thus determined to retain charge of her own property. When Lizzie and Hezekiah Williams started up the Chisholm Trail sometime in the 1880s, Williams accompanied her husband to watch over her own cows. They drove a buggy while cowhands moved the cattle north. Covering about ten miles a day, Williams enjoyed the adventure of the trail as well as the cowboys' attention. They lavished her with gifts such as wild fruit, prairie chicken, and antelope tongue, and Williams often recounted the times when the cowboys put a rope around Hezekiah's and her bedroll to deter rattlesnakes.

Although Williams died a lonely, miserly lady, with diamonds and money stashed in dark corners of her house, she eluded hanging. Today, she is remembered as the "Queen of Ranching," who made a fortune through her business.

The stories of women who trailed cattle helped spread the word that cowgirls not only existed but worked cattle as a vocation. Margaret Borland of Victoria, Texas acquired her husband's herd after his death and drove them over the Chisholm Trail. Mrs. Nat Collins of Montana accompanied her cattle from Choteau, Montana to the Chicago market in the fall of 1891; for this feat she was named "Cattle Queen of Montana." Newlyweds Mary Taylor Bunton and her husband rode up the Chisholm Trail in 1886, just before the overland drives ended. Mary Bunton rode in a Concord buggy part of the way but preferred to ride her cream-colored, Spanish pony sidesaddle alongside the cattle. She wore a green riding habit with a long skirt and took her turn as a regular hand much of the time. Since her habit was progressively shredded, the cowboys remarked that they could easily follow the herd by the fragments of the green skirt.

Mary Ann Goodnight, the second ranch woman in the Texas Panhandle, assisted her husband, the renowned Charles Goodnight, on a cattle drive in 1877

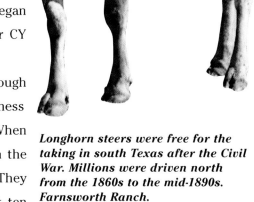

Longhorn steers were free for the taking in south Texas after the Civil War. Millions were driven north from the 1860s to the mid-1890s. Farnsworth Ranch.

This photograph features a triumphant cowgirl who, like the cowboys, packs iron and ropes steers on the prairie. As a concession to the Victorian rules, she has draped a hide over her pants to look more ladylike. Naramore Collection.

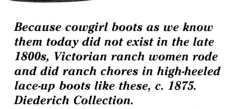

Ranch women in the late 1800s rode sidesaddle in long, full skirts and dressed more elegantly than one would perhaps expect. As ranch woman Sue Sanders wrote about the Civil War period, "At that time such a thing as a lady showing an ankle or an inch of leg was a bounded disgrace." Diederich Collection.

Because cowgirl boots as we know them today did not exist in the late 1800s, Victorian ranch women rode and did ranch chores in high-heeled lace-up boots like these, c. 1875. Diederich Collection.

A petite size and a feminine stitched pattern indicate that these high-tops are an early pair of cowgirl boots, c. 1890. The stitching on the boots protected legs from chafing on the stirrup leathers and provided protection from livestock kicks. Holley Collection.

from Pueblo, Colorado to her new home in Palo Duro Canyon. She drove the supply wagons and was in charge of the outfit in her husband's absence. John Adair of England drove cattle with his wife Cornelia, who won the admiration of all the cowboys for riding the entire distance of four hundred miles on horseback. Henrietta Chamberlain, who married millionaire rancher Richard King of Texas, also helped her husband and was known to ride on round-ups and drives. Possibly the high profile of these socially-prominent women helped ranch work become more acceptable for members of the fairer sex.

Masculine jobs and ranching became more commonplace for women as more people moved West, because settling the frontier and homesteading land required everyone's help. Some women found homesteading lonely and too difficult; others welcomed the rigorous lifestyle for the rewards of fresh air and hard work.

In the fall of 1889, newlyweds Evelyn and Ewen Cameron traveled from Great Britain to the Badlands of eastern Montana Territory to enjoy a hunting trip. They discovered a sparsely-populated landscape, settled by a few horse, cattle, and sheep ranches and filled with an "intense solitude," as Ewen Cameron described in a diary entry.

The couple decided to settle on this mysterious land because they found freedom in their distance from Great Britain, where Evelyn Cameron's family disapproved of her husband, who was older, eccentric, and financially insecure.

Born on an estate near the town of Streatham, just south of London, Cameron was the daughter of a wealthy and prestigious merchant of the East India Co. At the age of twenty-one, she turned her back on the world of English country houses and London parties for the peace she felt on her ranch, far from the scrutiny of her family and English society. Her high-spirited nature suited the Badlands, a place which she felt lacked pretense and formality.

Cameron also relished the work. In one letter to her family, she expressed no desire for help:

"No, I have no servant and I do all my own house work and infinitely prefer doing it and being independent of 'hired help'." She later added. . . "manual labor is about all I care about and, after all, is what will really make a strong woman. I like to break colts, brand calves, cut down trees, ride and work in the garden."

Cameron also dehorned calves, "using only lye and a penknife," and broke horses. She was especially proud of the latter skill. Even at temperatures of forty and fifty degrees below zero, she worked outside.

One afternoon, Cameron's neighboring rancher, James Whaley, ran into her yard in a state of desperation. The Yellowstone River was flooding, and his cows, having wandered into the river bottom, were drowning. Horrified, Cameron hurried to the scene and, wearing her bathing suit, jumped into the water. She swam against strong currents to rescue a dozen calves. Later she

High-top laced cowgirl boots with flat heels were practical for riding and simple ranch work. Spurs, like this California pair made by Jesus Tapia, c. 1900, easy to identify with his trademark silver "nipple" buttons, were typically worn. High Noon Collection.

Because ranchers lived considerable distances from stores, they often made do with what was available. A woman wore this long-shanked pair of August Buermann iron spurs on a pair of mining boots, c. 1915. Prairie Rose Collection.

discovered that her feet were punctured with thorns from a thick rose bush under the flood waters.

Cameron also pulled cows. On rare occasions her husband, who spent much of his days studying birds, helped with the ranch work. In one diary entry she wrote:

"To barn, found Starlight. . . [with] her calf's head and fore feet appearing. I pulled and pulled. Ewen had to help & we got it out only attached by umbilical cord. It would have suffocated if we hadn't drawn it out, the vagina compressed its lungs so."

After her husband died, Cameron continued to run the ranch alone and resisted the modern world. "I will never own a motor as long as I can throw my leg over a saddle," she said. She found adventure and peace in her life without electricity or running water, and she encouraged others to chose her lifestyle. In a letter to a friend in England she wrote:

"You can help me pitch hay, feed chickens ects.! These are the tonics that will make you feel the world is not such a bad place after all." She added in a later note: "What lovely, pure, exhilarating air this is in Montana. It would cure many nervous and other ills if it was only given the chance."

Most women who followed their husbands West and were expected to participate in everything from washing dishes to branding cattle to scaring off Indians remain unheralded. Mary A. Blankenship of Texas wrote about her ranch chores in her book, *The West Is For Us*: "The pioneer

Cotton bandanas of various designs, c. 1900, served a score of practical functions. Schmitt/Cayuse Collection.

This painting by W. Herbert Dunton features a cowgirl wearing a bandana and outfitted in classic western clothing of the early 1900s.

Elsie Cooksley (later Lloyd), age twenty (left) and Amy Cooksley (later Chubb), age seventeen arrived in Wyoming in 1914 with their parents from England. After several years, they moved to a ranch, where the two daughters rode horses, put up hay, and managed the cattle. As the only two women on local round-ups, they said that they were treated with respect.

W. Herbert Dunton

Mabel Strong, probably a Wild West show performer, wears a pair of leggings. Schmitt/Cayuse Collection.

These riding leggings are highly decorated with leather overlays and elaborate stitching, c. 1900. High Noon Collection.

woman of the prairie soon sacrificed her femininity as she laid away her frills for the plain living, and took upon herself the yoke beside her husband as a team-mate and companion, forever at his side whether it was on a saddle, cultivator, go-devil, binder, pulling a cotton sack, hunting, pitching bundles, or stacking feed, and all of this in addition to the housekeeping and preserving food. Our day was from daylight till dark."

Often men left women alone on ranches when they went to retrieve stock. During these times women fended for themselves, with a gun if necessary. "There's a gun in every corner of the cabin," said one Texas cowboy to his bride. Because ranches were so remote, women had to learn to confront hardship and to be independent and self-sufficient.

In the early 1900s, Alice Stillwell married a Texas rancher who expected her to help with ranch work. When she walked into the one-room shack that was to be her new home, the cowboys predicted: "Hell, that woman school teacher won't last six months down here in this godforsaken country." Alice Stillwell wondered herself if she would survive as she looked around the small room furnished with a cookstove, a blackened coffee pot, a

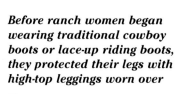

Before ranch women began wearing traditional cowboy boots or lace-up riding boots, they protected their legs with high-top leggings worn over

Victorian shoes. Some carried western decoration, seen here as a brass Texas Star, c. 1890. Schmitt/Cayuse Collection.

26

huge black iron teakettle, and a few pots and pans. There was a cabinet with a shelf accommodating a water bucket and gourd dipper. One table, one chair, two wooden benches, and one bedroll—a mass of rolled-up quilts wrapped in a tarp in a corner—also embellished the room.

"I reckon you'll be a goin' back to town most of the time," one hand said to her as he gathered the tin plates and crude silverware to wash.

"No, I expect to live here with Roy, or I wouldn't have married him," Stillwell replied.

"It's no fittin' place for a woman," mumbled another hand.

But Stillwell's husband expected her to work with him and she soon learned to love herding cattle, taking care of the calves, and housekeeping on the range. In her book, *I'll Gather My Geese*, she wrote about their second ranch in the high country:

"As we rode up to Dove Mountain Place, I felt that I had indeed come to the jumping-off place at the end of the world. I somehow knew that I would never be the same again. I found out quickly that I was to live like a man, work like a man, and act like a man, and I was not so sure I was not a man when it was all over. The Good Lord did give me a mind that could not be governed by a man, and I remained a woman. I feel sure at times now that this one fact caused me lots of grief, but also lots of happiness."

Eva Antonia Wilbur-Cruce, a turn-of-the-century rancher's daughter from Arizona, called the West a beautiful, cruel country, but her spirit seemed to thrive on this juxtaposition. Perhaps her words best describe the vitality that these early ranch women gained from their connection to the western landscape. "I have never felt depressed or lonely when alone with the land," Wilbur-Cruce wrote. "Something always happens that dazzles me and overwhelms me with amazement and wonder." The early cowgirl, now working outside the home, seemed to blossom as she confronted challenge, sought adventure, and discovered solace in the sagebrush-covered, open spaces. Her spirit thrived on its connection to a beautiful, cruel country.

(top) **This 101 Ranch cowgirl, who probably worked cattle as well as performed, sports the style of a rodeo cowgirl with her big hat and bow, fringed riding skirt, leather cuffs, and arm bands. National Cowgirl Museum and Hall of Fame.**

Mabel Miller, Zach Miller's wife, worked on the 101 Ranch in a conversion skirt and a man's style shirt. National Cowboy Hall of Fame.

BORN WESTERN

Unlike their mothers, the children of the early cowgirls were simply born into lives on the ranch and range. Most cowgirls and cowboys learned to ride and rope because these activities were part of their chores as ranch offspring. Renowned rodeo cowgirl Fanny Sperry Steele, born in Montana in 1897, rode her first pony at six (actually late for many ranch girls) and was henceforth expected to break her own horses. Lucille Mulhall, who became a leading Wild West show and rodeo performer, also learned her skills on a ranch. Like many other young ranch girls, she was expected to pull her own weight alongside her father and brothers. Mulhall's father told Lucille she could have as many cattle as she could rope and brand. After she proved her proficiency at this task, he asked her to stop for fear she would deprive him of all his cattle.

For children, ranching was a life full of both hard work and adventure. They chased the wind across pastures and spent a considerable portion of their day with animals, domesticated and wild. Agnes Morley Cleaveland remembers parading around her family's ranch in New Mexico with her brothers and sisters, Spotty the young fawn, Smarty the goat and foster mother to the fawn, Bobby the cat, Buffalo Bill the rooster, and Josh, a three-month-old black bear.

"For us children, . . . the new life was from the beginning a sort of glorified picnic," wrote Cleaveland in her book *No Life For A Lady*. Born in 1874, she spent most of her life working with the cowboys and helping her family run the ranch. "I worked side by side with the men, receiving the same praise or same censure for like undertakings," she wrote. "I can still hear Bowlegs scoffing at me because a 'longear' got away from me in the brush. What kind of brush rider was I that I couldn't keep close enough to a yearling to see which way it went?"

Montana ranch women of the 1920s and 1930s Alice and Margie Greenough also learned to ride and work beside their father and brothers. Outside chores took priority over inside chores, because the survival of the family required their help. No one could afford to raise

Ranch girls were born to the saddle. This young cowgirl takes her first ride on grandpa's knee, c. 1905. Museum of New Mexico Collection.

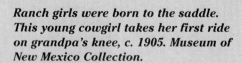

Cowgirls learned to ride alongside their fathers and brothers. A Montana cowgirl named Norma Sauke Thornton worked outside with her dad and never learned the homemaking skills required of girls her age. Horses became her "dolls" and working them her "play."

Young women were expected to help their fathers and brothers, and often-times their mothers, with ranch work. Stevenson Collection.

ladies that worked only in the house, attended teas, and welcomed visitors in the parlor. "We learned to ride horses before we could walk," Margie Greenough said. "Dad would give us a bucking horse and expect us to make a good horse out of him. If we bucked off, we better find him and bring him back home."

For young women who grew up ranching at the turn of the century, rodeo and Wild West shows presented an additional and viable way to make a living with the horsemanship skills they already possessed. When the Greenough sisters heard they could make a living riding in rodeos, they went to their father to announce their departure. Pack Saddle Ben Greenough knew that stopping his girls was futile. "You have more guts than good sense, anyway, so go on," he said. "Just take Old Willy with you." Old Willy was the Greenough name for willpower.

Confident and highly skilled, ranch girls moved into the show arena. Like the cowboys, they sought both money and fame. In the process, challenge and glory fed their souls.

For many of the children, riding a horse or a mule on a ranch was an adventure. Parents often pulled children out of school to help with important ranch chores, c. 1895. Colorado Historical Society.

SPLIT SKIRTS & SIDESADDLES

The first cowgirl clothes and saddles were unsuitable. Despite her considerable skill and spirit, a Victorian horsewoman wore a long skirt (sometimes with a bustle) and a blouse with tall collar and long sleeves. Without question, she rode sidesaddle. Ever since Anne of Bohemia, wife of Richard II, introduced the sidesaddle to Europeans in 1382, it was considered unladylike to ride astride. Despite notable exceptions, for hundreds of years women rode sideways to show off long gowns; even Napoleon rode sidesaddle on special occasions. From the 1880s through the early 1900s, cowgirls as well as other American women challenged conventional riding styles.

Evelyn Cameron was discouraged to find that dresses and sidesaddles made it impossible for her to ride a spirited bronc:

"It was my unfortunate experience that nearly all the horses I wished to ride were terrified of a woman in a riding habit," she wrote in 1914, "and when their fears were sufficiently subdued to admit of my approach near enough to mount, they declined to allow me to do so. Even when I was assisted to the saddle by several men, the horse 'threw a fit' as I raised my leg to put it over the pommel, and, of course, I had the same trouble in dismounting. It was clear that to be perfectly independent I must ride old 'dead heads,' which were not at all to my taste."

For some time, western women put up with the cumbersome skirts and accompanying sidesaddle. To the horror of the Indians, who believed she was a strange creature with one leg, Narcissa Prentiss Whitman rode the Oregon Trail in 1836 on a sidesaddle. Other women rode on round-ups or to town, and a

Before the acceptance of the split riding skirt, many women wore large prairie skirts that were extra-long in the back and could be skirted up between the legs for riding astride. This hand-made skirt of calf skin was owned by a working cowgirl in California, c. 1880. Schmitt/ Cayuse Collection.

This ranch woman rides with a prairie skirt in the astride position, a practice considered unladylike in the 1880s.

(opposite) *Photographer Evelyn Cameron, who thrived on the ranch life and fresh air of Montana, took this self-portrait in 1912. Montana Historical Society and Photographing Montana 1894-1928.*

This sidesaddle from the Civil War period features an extremely large skirt on the near side and a carpet-faced rear saddle pad. Birds, goblets, and flowers were hand-painted in red and green on the engraved leather. Sage Collection.

Early ranch women and visitors attended round-ups and rode sidesaddle in cumbersome English riding habits well into the early 1900s. Often ladies rode sidesaddle to a dance fifty miles from their ranch with their silk dress folded in a small bag hanging from the horn. Lebel Collection.

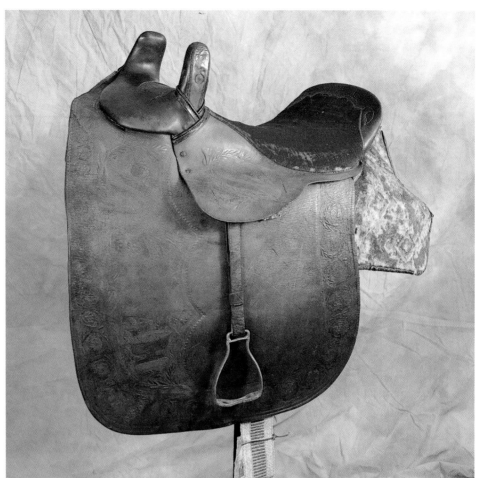

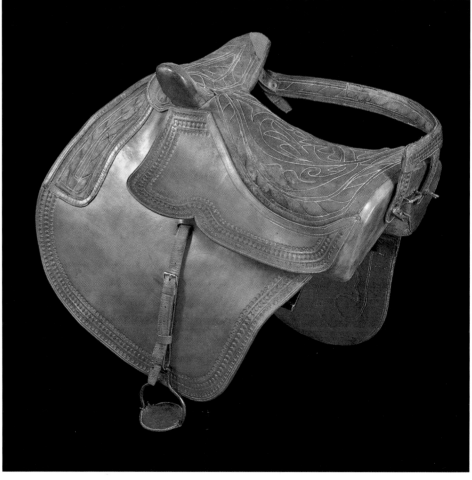

Sidesaddle with suede, quilted seat and kneeroll, and a backbar affording additional security for the rider. A secure pouch and the lady's initials "NG" are prominent features on the off (right) side, c. 1890. Sage Collection.

This sidesaddle with an embroidered, quilted seat was made by Clark, a commercial saddlery based in Portland, Oregon, c. 1895-1905. Fleischer Collection.

Even in such rustic locations as the prairies of Alberta, women were expected to ride sidesaddle. Many even continued to wear corsets. This woman poses for a photograph, c. 1885. Glenbow Archives.

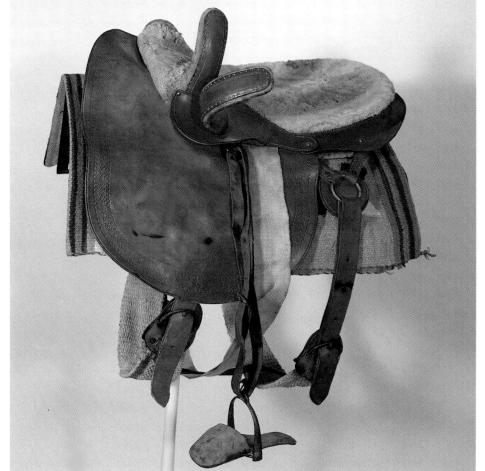

An 1880s sidesaddle, featuring a slipper stirrup, made by J.S. Collins of Cheyenne, Wyoming. Fleischer Collection.

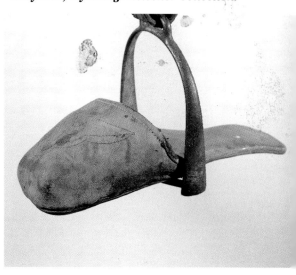

33

Mrs. Riordan even rode broncs in a sidesaddle at the Cheyenne Frontier Days rodeo at the turn of the century.

With slight variations, sidesaddles in the United States around the close of the nineteenth century can be grouped into three distinct styles. Sidesaddles from the Civil War era had a large square skirt on the near (left) side, which prevented a women's skirt from mixing with horse sweat and hair. The right leg rested between two horns, the lower serving as a "post" around which the knee was bent. One stirrup, which replaced the old plancette, or footrest, accomodated the woman's left foot. These saddles were surprisingly balanced. If a lady sat properly in her seat, her weight was evenly distributed over the horse's back.

The second style of sidesaddle resembled an English saddle with rounded skirts, two horns, a stirrup, and one girth. A third horn (called a "leaping horn") was added early in the nineteenth century by a team of Frenchmen. This extra horn, which could be screwed into the saddle, curved over the left thigh and provided the equestrienne more security when she jumped or galloped across uneven country on a fox hunt. These saddles were frequently made with quilted seats which were stuffed with horsehair and featured ornate stitching. Many of these sidesaddles found their way out West.

As more women populated the West, saddleries like R.T. Frazier (Pueblo, Colorado), F.A. Meanea (Cheyenne, Wyoming), Hamley (Pendleton, Oregon), and H.H. Heiser (Denver, Colorado), recognizing a demand for ladies' saddles, designed a "western" sidesaddle. More like a stock saddle with its square skirts

This western horsewoman exhibits plenty of style in her classic sidesaddle outfit of the 1890s. A Mrs. Minta Holmsley of Comanche country said women rode up the cattle trails on sidesaddles "because we didn't have any better sense." Holley Collection.

A true "working" sidesaddle, showing the third leaping horn (bottom horn), double rigging, and overgirth, c. 1890. Sage Collection.

(right) May Lillie, wife of Pawnee Bill, rode sidesaddle throughout her life. She is shown here in 1930 on their Oklahoma ranch. Circus World Museum.

Western sidesaddles were double-rigged for both a front and rear cinch, a design that provided greater stability on rugged terrain. This sidesaddle was made by T. Row of Austin, Texas, c. 1900, for a member of the Ringling family (Ringling Bros. Circus). The saddle is ornately carved with floral decoration and includes a small saddle pocket on the off side. Benson Collection.

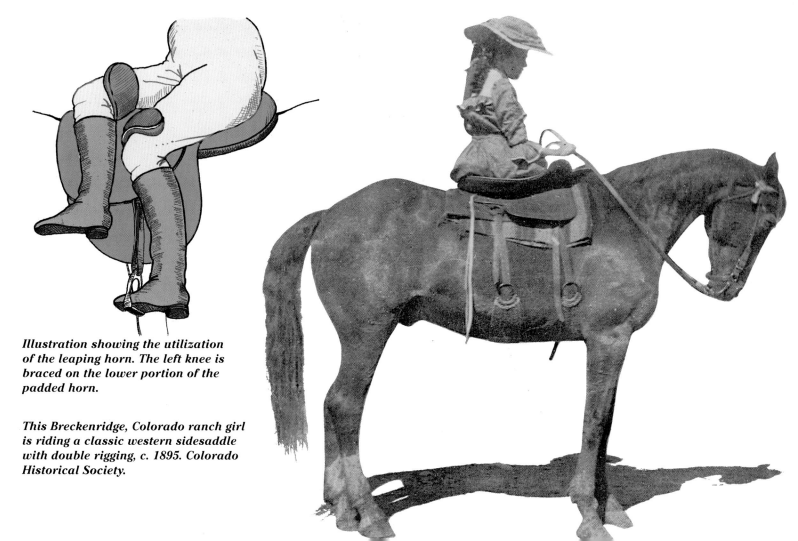

Illustration showing the utilization of the leaping horn. The left knee is braced on the lower portion of the padded horn.

This Breckenridge, Colorado ranch girl is riding a classic western sidesaddle with double rigging, c. 1895. Colorado Historical Society.

and double rigging, this saddle was more substantial than the English variety and always sported three horns. Although the leaping horn had existed for nearly forty years, its invention is sometimes attributed to distinguished Texas trail driver and rancher Charles Goodnight, who designed one of the first western sidesaddles for his wife. In 1870, he commissioned S.C. Gallup in Pueblo, Colorado to make a western sidesaddle which had a square skirt, double rigging, slipper tapadero stirrup, a wide, comfortable buckskin seat, and lavish tooled designs.

The popular "catalog" saddles generally lacked the tooled work, and carpet seats were typical. In 1897, the Sears, Roebuck, and Co. catalog offered twenty-one different sidesaddle styles. If a woman was unable to find a sidesaddle, she rode the standard man's stock saddle with her leg hooked over the horn.

Riding sideways soon grew tiresome. The long skirt was cumbersome, easily caught on brush, and frankly dangerous; the sidesaddle was a precarious perch from which to rope a steer or chase cattle. Early western women were some of the first females to challenge this impractical tradition.

On the advice of the ranch manager, Evelyn Cameron sent away to a well-known Chicago firm for what was called a California riding costume, which cost her one hundred dollars. The skirt was long but split like pants to allow her to ride like a man. When she rode the forty-eight miles from her ranch into Miles City, Montana in her California riding habit, folks were shocked. "It created a small sensation," Cameron said. "So great at first was the prejudice against any divided garment in Montana that a warning was given me to abstain from riding on the streets of Miles City lest I might be arrested!"

The split riding skirt was a solution to a ranch woman's dilemma. By unbuttoning the front panel she could easily ride astride and perform ranch chores. When she dismounted she could button up the front panel and stroll through town in ladylike fashion. This heavy twill style was popular in the 1890s. Schmitt/Cayuse Collection.

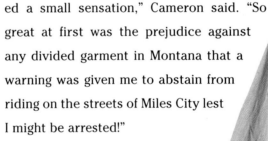

Slowly, however, cowgirls who rode astride earned acceptance. In December, 1906, *The Ladies Home Journal* stated: "Many young girls are now taught to ride cross-saddle, as the old-style of sidesaddle riding is thought to make a girl become crooked." How interesting that the Victorian side-

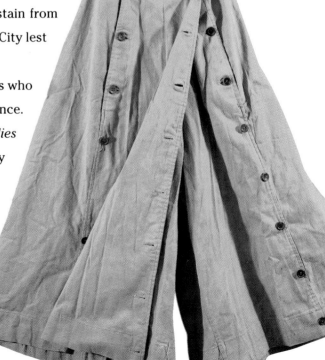

Janet Williams with her horse Zip on the Yellowstone River in 1911. Williams was photographed by her friend, Evelyn Cameron. Montana Historical Society & Photographing Montana 1894-1928.

Cowgirl images appeared on a variety of products. This brass coin purse is decorated with a cowgirl and her pony, c. 1905. Schmitt/Cayuse Collection.

By 1905 the split riding skirt had become the standard uniform for young ranch women. They could travel virtually anywhere as "ladies." This illustration depicts the independent cowgirl, alone with her pony in a high mountain meadow. DeBeer Collection.

As cowgirls developed more style, they demanded riding skirts with a true western flair. This leather skirt, made by C.P. Shipley, c. 1910, is decorated with brass spots in a star and heart pattern on the waistband and sports abundant fringe. Williams Collection.

saddle was designed for and made popular by Queen Elizabeth to mask in part her physical deformities!

Perhaps Agnes Morley Cleaveland described best the disregard for lady-like behavior and the ardor with which the cowgirl discarded her Victorian trappings: "My own great concession to a new age was to abandon the sidesaddle. Why, for ten years, I continued to ride sidesaddle is a mystery to me now. I recall the steps that led to emancipation," she wrote in *No Life for a Lady*.

"First I discarded, or rather refused to adopt, the sunbonnet, conventional headgear of my female neighbors. When I went unashamedly about under a five-gallon (not ten-gallon) Stetson, many an eyebrow was raised; then followed a double-breasted blue flannel shirt, with white pearl buttons, frankly unfeminine. In time came blue denim knickers worn under a short blue denim skirt. Slow evolution (or was it decadence?) toward a costume suited for immediate needs. Decadence having set in, the descent from the existing standards of female modesty to purely human comfort and convenience was swift. A man's saddle and a divided skirt (awful monstrosity that was) were inevitable. This was the middle nineties."

Acceptance was neither swift nor immediate.

"I won't ride in the same canyon with you," protested Cleaveland's brother Ray, when she first appeared astride and wearing a split skirt.

Anna Hanson riding on the Horn Ranch in 1905 near Boham, Texas. She is wearing a broad-brimmed Stetson hat and her split riding skirt. Edwin E. Smith photo, Amon Carter Museum.

A cowgirl belt buckle made by Eddy Hulbert for the Bischoff family of Kane, Wyoming. Created in the late 1940s or early 1950s, this sterling and gold buckle features a cowgirl's initials and her ranch brand. Schmitt/Cayuse Collection.

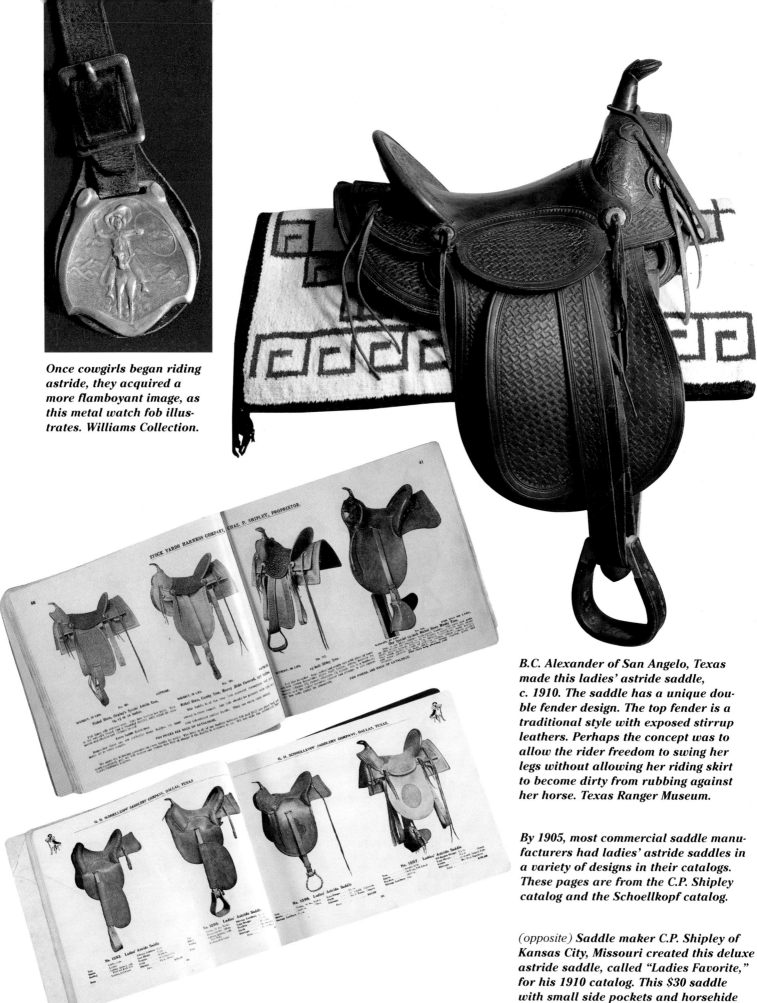

Once cowgirls began riding astride, they acquired a more flamboyant image, as this metal watch fob illustrates. Williams Collection.

B.C. Alexander of San Angelo, Texas made this ladies' astride saddle, c. 1910. The saddle has a unique double fender design. The top fender is a traditional style with exposed stirrup leathers. Perhaps the concept was to allow the rider freedom to swing her legs without allowing her riding skirt to become dirty from rubbing against her horse. Texas Ranger Museum.

By 1905, most commercial saddle manufacturers had ladies' astride saddles in a variety of designs in their catalogs. These pages are from the C.P. Shipley catalog and the Schoellkopf catalog.

(opposite) *Saddle maker C.P. Shipley of Kansas City, Missouri created this deluxe astride saddle, called "Ladies Favorite," for his 1910 catalog. This $30 saddle with small side pockets and horsehide trimming weighed only twenty-two pounds. Hengesbaugh Collection.*

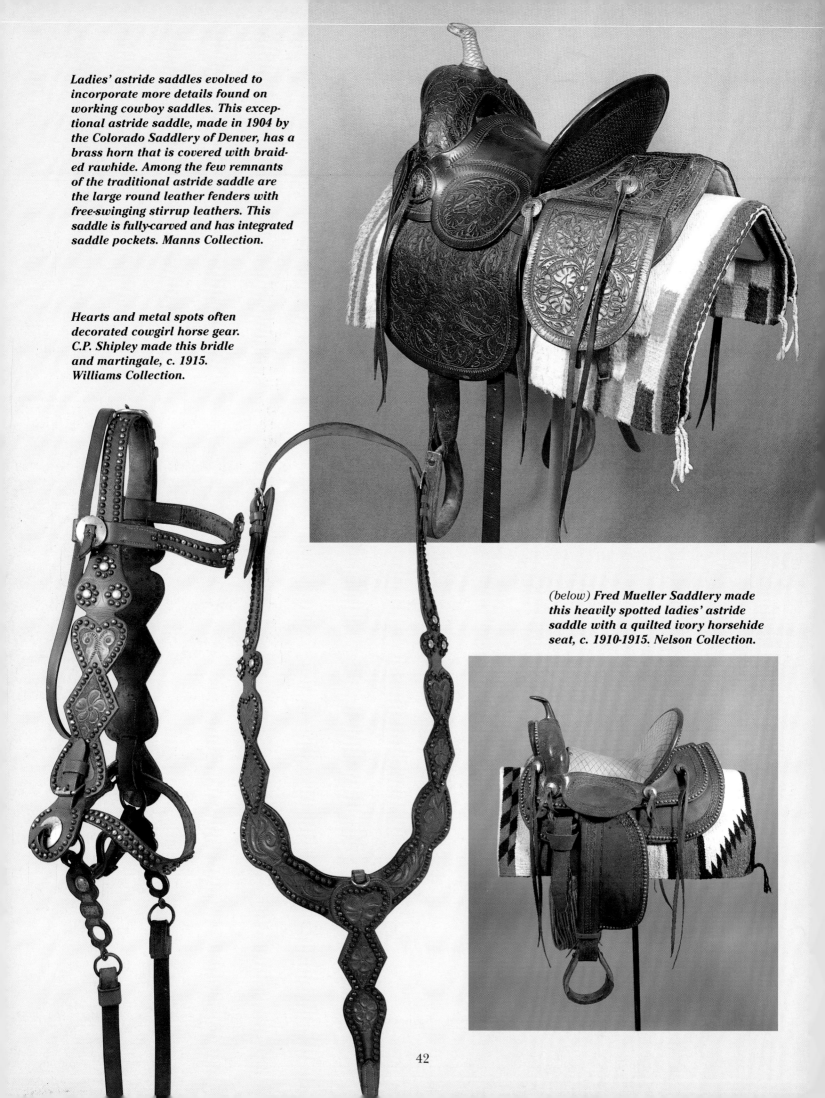

Ladies' astride saddles evolved to incorporate more details found on working cowboy saddles. This exceptional astride saddle, made in 1904 by the Colorado Saddlery of Denver, has a brass horn that is covered with braided rawhide. Among the few remnants of the traditional astride saddle are the large round leather fenders with free-swinging stirrup leathers. This saddle is fully-carved and has integrated saddle pockets. Manns Collection.

Hearts and metal spots often decorated cowgirl horse gear. C.P. Shipley made this bridle and martingale, c. 1915. Williams Collection.

(below) Fred Mueller Saddlery made this heavily spotted ladies' astride saddle with a quilted ivory horsehide seat, c. 1910-1915. Nelson Collection.

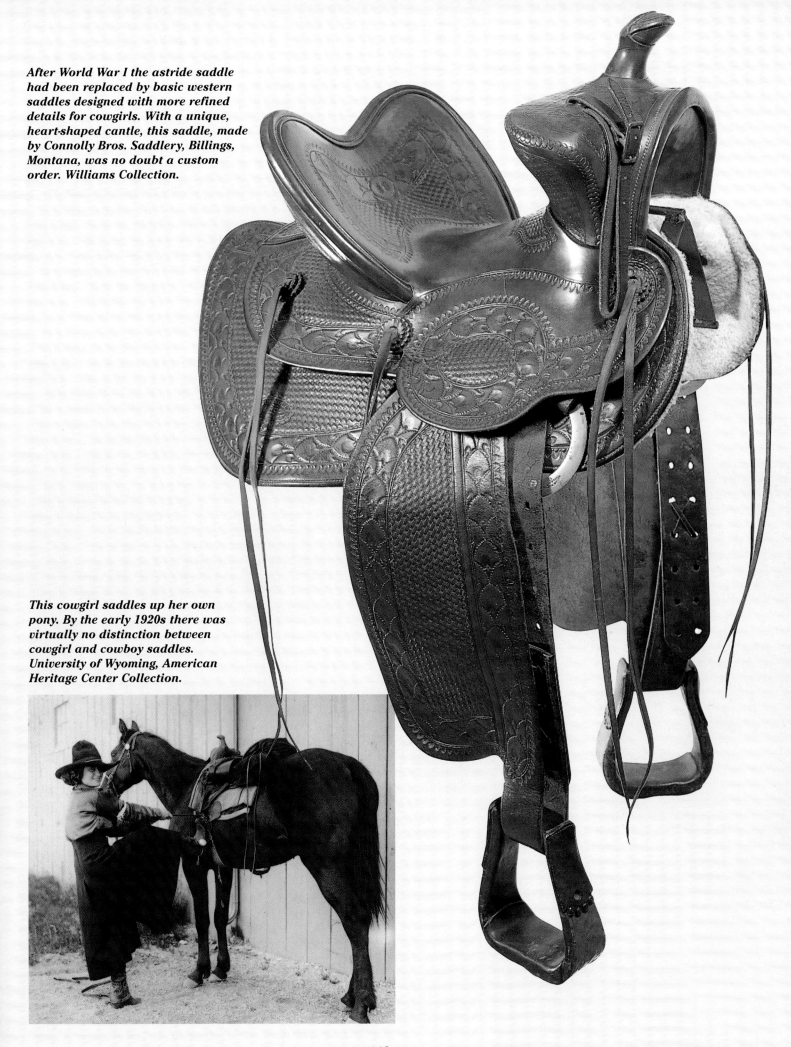

After World War I the astride saddle had been replaced by basic western saddles designed with more refined details for cowgirls. With a unique, heart-shaped cantle, this saddle, made by Connolly Bros. Saddlery, Billings, Montana, was no doubt a custom order. Williams Collection.

This cowgirl saddles up her own pony. By the early 1920s there was virtually no distinction between cowgirl and cowboy saddles. University of Wyoming, American Heritage Center Collection.

(right) *As cowgirls took on more rigorous ranch work, they began wearing chaps. This woman wears white Angora woolly chaps (shown below) on her father's S bar B Dude Ranch in Cameron, Montana, c. 1930. Sage Collection.*

On northern ranches of Montana and Wyoming, woolly chaps were part of the standard uniform during winter months. This working cowgirl poses for a photograph, c. 1912. Schmitt/Cayuse Collection.

By the mid-1920s dude ranch cowgirls were wearing flashy, spotted, batwing-style chaps. This pair has over 2,000 nickel-plated brass harness spots. Lebel Collection.

Shotgun-style chaps were conical sleeves of leather typically decorated with fringe and metal conchas. This pair, made by the Visalia Stock Saddle Company in California, was a custom order for a cowgirl to accommodate a woman's hips. c. 1920. Wideman Collection.

This dude girl (late 1920s) sports an expensive pair of batwing chaps with ornate contrasting leather overlays. Few working cowgirls would have worn anything this fancy or heavy. Schmitt/Cayuse Collection.

(right) *Idaho cowgirl Gertrude Maxwell's silver overlay spurs made by Qualey Bros., c. 1930. Maxwell's last initial and the maker mark appear on the outside heel band. The Qualeys were Norwegian immigrants who homesteaded on the Joseph Plains of Idaho in 1915. Brothers Tom and Nels learned spurmaking from their father Knut. For decades they made spurs for the local ranchers in central Idaho. Schmitt/Cayuse Collection.*

(above) *Cowgirl spurs were typically petite and ornate. This pair, featuring petal-style rowels, was created by the Visalia Stock Saddle Company shortly after the turn of the century. Statler Collection.*

(right) *Most commercial spur manufacturers produced spurs in standard patterns but on a smaller scale for cowgirls. C.P. Shipley of Kansas City, Missouri fashioned these spurs, c. 1920, with a "snowflake" rowel. Wideman Collection.*

Cowgirls in California wore spurs that were extremely ornate with intricate silver inlays, c. 1895-1915. California-style spurs were inspired by classic Mexican designs. High Noon Collection.

Double-mounted McChesney spurs with silver heart buttons, a variation of the ladies' no. 23 spur in the no. 9 catalog, c. 1916. The spurs are brass and silver and feature a standard rowel. Schmitt/Cayuse Collection.

Like many cowboys, cowgirls in their western finery posed for photographers, as seen in this studio photo, c. 1890s. Walden Collection.

This cowgirl from the southwest poses in a fringed dress, straw hat, and leather gauntlets. Her Colt Single Action with a 7½ inch barrel hangs low off her hip in typical cowgirl fashion. During the last three decades of the 1800s, women were prepared to defend themselves if necessary. Manns Collection.

Three ranch women with their guns posed for this picture, c. 1900-1905. Slaughter Collection.

A calender photo featuring a cowgirl with a cartridge belt and gun. Packing iron out West was not unusual for women in the 1890s. High Noon Collection.

This photograph, c. 1910, was included in a package of Hanssan Cigarettes along with other images of cowboy life. Lipman Collection.

QUEEN OF THE RANCH

Cowboys and cowgirls often worked together on the range at the turn of the century. This cowgirl wears her Colt six-shooter in a cross-draw fashion. Montana Historical Society.

Dressed in a buckskin riding skirt and packing a Colt Single Action with a 7½ inch barrel, this cowgirl was prepared for life on the range. Women in the West learned to be comfortable with guns. Pioneer Mrs. Blankenship of Lubbock, Texas and her husband always slept with theirs. "The three of us and the shotgun shared the same feather bed," wrote a pregnant Blankenship of their first night on their new claim. Lebel Collection.

52

This home-made cowgirl skirt was probably worn with leggings or over pants.
The spotted gun belt and pearl-handled
Smith & Wesson .38 caliber revolver
resemble items that a female Wild West
show performer might have used.
Schmitt/Cayuse Collection.

Armed women on the frontier were not uncommon.
It was important to be able to defend oneself and
one's family and, if necessary, to signal for help
or dispatch incapacitated livestock.

53

LOOKING FOR GAME

While women in the West were accustomed to guns, travelers from the East would have found this 1910 postcard, showing a cowgirl on horseback with a rifle, a novelty. Schmitt/Cayuse Collection.

At her ranch on Black Thunder Creek in New Castle, Wyoming, Frances Mullin used her Colt Single Action to keep unwanted intruders out of her cabin. Woman were often left behind during round-ups and had to be prepared to defend themselves.

(above) Men as well as women packed into the mountains to hunt elk for winter sustenance. These two Wyoming women killed a bull elk in 1904 in northwestern Wyoming. Manns Collection.

(below) Gertrude Maxwell's Smith & Wesson double action, .38 caliber special, holster, and unmarked gun rig, c. 1920. National Cowgirl Museum and Hall of Fame.

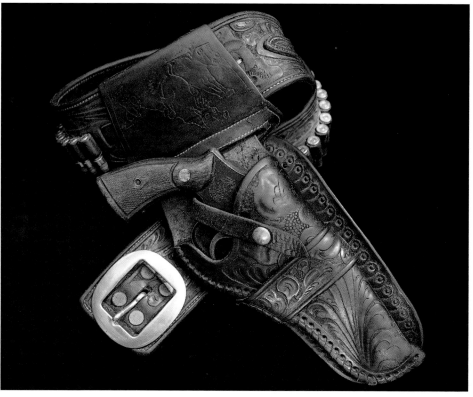

BAD GIRLS

Female outlaws out West were not considered cowgirls, but their rowdy behavior and disreputability contributed to the conception of the cowgirl as an undisciplined character. Dime novelists, journalists, sensationalists, and Hollywood writers seized the opportunity to glamorize notorious outlaws like Belle Starr, Calamity Jane, and Pearl Hart. Audiences worldwide devoured exaggerated tales of these lawless women and their felonious exploits. For the most part, western afficionados found these outlaw spirits endearing; their names became household words.

Because the media were so successful in their creation of the myths about the deeds of these bandit queens, the truth is difficult to ascertain. Unquestionably, all three women committed crimes, but the extent of their nefarious activities is less than legend would have one believe.

Belle Starr (born Myra Belle Shirley in 1848) was called the "Female Jesse James" and "The Petticoat Terror of the Plains." She was an excellent horsewoman, who rode sidesaddle, wore long skirts, and carried a Colt .45 which she called "my baby." As a young girl, Starr, who lived in Texas with her family, was a supporter of the Confederacy and once acted as a spy on her brother's behalf. After the war, both her friends and husbands were connected with outlaw gangs. In fact, it is believed that Cole Younger was the father of Starr's daughter Pearl. Although Starr was convicted of only one crime, the theft of a horse, she did mix with thieves and was murdered on February 3, 1889 for reasons unknown.

Calamity Jane (born Martha Jane Cannary in 1852) arrived in Montana as a teenager. Soon thereafter, her parents died, and she was forced to fend for herself. Wandering throughout the Dakotas, Colorado, Montana, and Wyoming, Jane consorted with miners, soldiers, and railroad workers. She accumulated numerous "husbands" and earned a reputation for helping the sick and the needy. Other occupations included bullwhacking, running a hurdy-gurdy house and a saloon, staking a few claims, waitressing, and appearing twice on stage. Sporting leather pants, fringed tops, and a gun, she acquired the name Calamity Jane at some point in her career.

Belle Starr, born Myra Belle Shirley, rides a sidesaddle and packs a "hog leg" in a Slim Jim-style holster. She was sensationalized in dime novels as the bandit queen. Her home on the Canadian river, called Younger Bend after her first love, was considered a refuge for many famous outlaws. Starr's most serious crime was stealing horses. Judge Parker, "the hanging judge" of Fort Smith, sentenced her to a year in prison in 1883. Starr loved adventure and had a soft spot for desperate men. She was shot in the back by an unknown assassin in 1889. University of Oklahoma, Western History.

A publicity shot of Calamity Jane as a scout for General Crook. Hundreds of these photos were sold to tourists. Her real name was Martha Cannary. She was born in Princeton, Missouri on May 1, 1852. Beginning in the early 1870s Cannary traveled throughout Wyoming and the Dakotas. She worked as a teamster and as an Army scout in 1872. Her unladylike exploits first appeared in a dime novel in 1877. These sensationalized western stories with titles such as "Calamity Jane, Queen of the Plains" and "Calamity Jane, The Heroine of Whoop-up" helped build her legend. She died in 1903 and was buried next to Wild Bill Hickok in Deadwood, South Dakota. National Cowgirl Museum and Hall of Fame.

Calamity Jane worked as a prostitute part time. Here are a few things she or one of her colleagues might have owned: a beaded holster, button opera boots, a garter dagger, business cards, and an opium pipe of carved ivory with a nude woman sitting on a pot and feeding a puppy. Holley Collection.

Because of her hard drinking and rowdy behavior, Calamity Jane spent much of her life in and out of jail. In 1896, she wrote *Life and Adventures*, an exaggerated but popular account of her exploits. She died in Terry, South Dakota on August 1, 1903. Although Calamity Jane was promiscuous as well as an alcoholic, most people prefer to remember her as a spirited Joan of Arc of the Plains or as the glamorous character played by actress Jean Arthur in *The Plainsman* (1936).

In 1899, Pearl Hart of Ontario, Canada, and her friend Joe Boot held up a stagecoach in Arizona. Wearing a rough miner's shirt and blue overalls, Hart stole $290 from a drummer, $36 from another male passenger, and $100 from a Chinese merchant. A nearby sheriff apprehended Hart and Boot and promptly took them to jail. Hart told the officials she robbed the stage because she needed money for her ailing mother. This story made headlines throughout the United States. Perhaps influenced by the publicity, the court acquitted Hart on November 25, 1899. The disgruntled judge tried Hart again for robbery and sentenced her to five years at the territorial prison in Yuma, Arizona, where the outlaw entertained curious visitors and wrote poetry. Although Boot received a sentence of thirty years, he escaped his prison cell and was never heard from again.

All three of these female outlaws live in the imagination as indominitable characters. Despite their criminal behavior and somewhat unsavory reputations, they have attained a level of immortality worldwide. Their exploits helped promote the idea that the West was not just a man's world and that there were female characters equally as wild and woolly as the men.

Pearl Hart holds a Winchester rifle. She became a celebrity while serving her five-year term at the territorial prison in Yuma, Arizona for robbing a stagecoach in 1899. Arizona Historical Society.

Cattle Annie and Little Britches, arrested in Oklahoma for cattle rustling, were sent to prison, c. 1880. Cattle Annie is holding a Winchester and Little Britches has a Colt Single Action revolver. University of Oklahoma, Western History.

Pearl Hart carried a Colt Thunderer revolver. Similar to the one carried by Billy The Kid, it was popular with women in the 1890s because of the small grip. Cervone Collection.

BUFFALO BILL'S WILD WEST.
CONGRESS, ROUGH RIDERS OF THE WORLD.

A. Hoen & Co., Baltimore, U.S.A.

MISS ANNIE OAKLEY,
THE PEERLESS LADY WING-SHOT.

WILD WEST

CHAPTER 2

In 1885, a girl in a wide-brimmed hat, fringed skirt, and jacket mounted her pinto pony in the shadows of a Chicago grandstand. A drum roll and trumpet call punctuated the announcer's staccato: "Ladies and gentlemen: The Honorable William F. Cody and Nathan Salsbury present the feature attraction, unique and unparalleled, the foremost woman marksman in the world, in an exhibition of skill with the rifle, shotgun, and pistol—the little girl of the Western plains—Annie Oakley!"

The young cowgirl charged into the arena and proceeded to shoot targets thrown by a cowboy on a galloping horse. Amid spontaneous applause, she sprang from her pony, ran towards her gun stand, and snatched up a rifle. Her husband Frank Butler juggled glass balls that shattered instantly in clouds of gunsmoke; no ball ever touched the ground. With a gleaming Bowie knife in one hand and her rifle in the other, Oakley next leapt onto a platform. Over her shoulder she aimed at a silver disk that Butler held over his head. Squinting into the knife blade, she eyed her target, fired, and watched the target spin from his hand. The crowd roared as this girl of the West swung into the saddle and galloped her pony out of the arena. Buffalo Bill grinned and hollered to her, "Sharp shooting, Missie!" as she disappeared with the last traces of gunsmoke.

This act was the beginning of Annie Oakley's career in show business, in which she became famous for her skill, daring, and beauty, a symbol of the Western woman's pioneer spirit. Oakley was not a damsel in distress. She was Little Sure Shot, nicknamed by Sitting Bull, the great Sioux chief who was also part of the show.

The incongruity of her marksmanship and lithe figure, as well as her modesty in the midst of gunsmoke, grizzled cowboys, and swarthy Indians, charmed audiences across the world. They stood amazed when this young

(opposite) **Annie Oakley, "peerless lady wing-shot", was one of the premiere attractions of Buffalo Bill's Wild West Show for seventeen seasons, c. 1890. Buffalo Bill Historical Center.**

Georgia Duffy, who wore a corset, was billed as the Rough Rider from Wyoming. She rode sidesaddle in Wild West shows during the late 1880s. University of Wyoming, American Heritage Center.

Buffalo Bill realized the importance of women performers. Many of the early rodeo stars began their careers in Cody's Wild West Show. Some of the most famous rodeo cowgirls are featured here in 1916 at the old Cubs ball park in Chicago during an open competition with the Miller Brothers' 101 Ranch Wild West Show. Back Row: Fanny Sperry Steele, unknown cowgirl, Bea Kirnan, Lucille Mulhall, unknown cowgirl, Edith Tantlinger with rope, Georgia Mulhall on horse. Front Row: LuLu Parr, Louise Thompson, Buffalo Bill, Vera McGinnis. Schmitt/Cayuse Collection.

Audiences were thrilled to see cowgirls performing traditional cowboy activities such as roping and riding wild horses. Circus World Museum.

woman with the star on her upturned hat extinguished with a single bullet the cigarette that Prince Wilhelm held in his mouth; punctured playing cards in her husband's hand, or shot out flames from a revolving wheel. A French count bowed, kissed her hand, and proposed marriage. An English sportsman wanted her to become mistress of his estate. A Welshman sent her his picture with a solemn proposal. She put the picture on a post, shot six holes through the man's eyes, and sent it back with the reply, "respectfully declined." Flowers and gifts filled her tent. Dressed in divided skirts, top boots, and wide, gray felt Stetson hats, Oakley and her peers "make a picture of femininity quite new to this country," wrote a reporter from the *London Daily Citizen.*

Born in Darke County, Ohio in 1860, Anne Moses grew up shooting rabbits, turkeys, wild geese, pigeons, grouse, and quail for the family dinner table. She used her father's long-barreled cap-and-ball Pennsylvania rifle and sold her extra birds to a trapper who owned a store in town. One afternoon, while visiting her sister and brother-in-law in Cincinnati, young Anne Moses impressed some members of a prestigious shooting club to the extent that they matched her with expert marksman Frank Butler at Shooter's Hill. She won the contest. Butler, charmed by this graceful girl, recognized her as having unusual skill; he married her one

Engraved receiver plate detail from Annie Oakley's model 1892 Winchester. Buffalo Bill Historical Center.

Annie Oakley never considered herself a trick shot; rather she saw herself as an expert marksman.

The Sioux chief Sitting Bull toured with Buffalo Bill in 1885. He was so impressed by Annie Oakley that he adopted her as a member of the tribe and gave her the name "Little Sure Shot." Buffalo Bill Memorial Museum.

May Manning was a Philadelphia girl and a graduate of Smith College who married western showman Gordon Lillie, better known as Pawnee Bill, in 1886. After discovering that she was unable to have a family, May Lillie threw herself into learning how to ride, rope, and shoot. She performed with her husband for the next quarter century.
She is shown rearing her horse while riding side-saddle in 1908.

year later. Within six years she had changed her name and had become a star. As her manager, Butler continued to support her act and remained devoted to his Annie Oakley until his death.

For the most part, Wild West shows like Buffalo Bill's, as well as nearly 120 others such as Pawnee Bill's Wild West and the Miller Brothers' 101 Ranch, brought the frontier culture to the doorstep of the Victorians. Thousands were awed by these shows—a feast of shooting, riding, cowboys, and Indians. There were painted backdrops of the Rocky Mountains, herds of buffalo transported to New York City, London, and Paris, cowboys, cowgirls, and Indians dressed in authentic costumes. Stagecoach robberies, Indian assaults, Custer's last stand, and rodeo events entertained audiences.

Many other shows featured women sharpshooters. Annie Oakley, May Lillie, "the champion girl shot of the West," and Princess Wenona, "the peerless horseback rifle shot," took the spotlight. These women often opened the program to ease the audience into what was for many an evening of culture shock. It was these young women who fueled people's imagination about the cowgirl.

Later, cowgirls were featured on bucking broncs and as trick-riders and fancy-ropers. Emma Hitchcock performed with her trick horse in a square dance in Buffalo Bill's Wild West Show. Like the sharpshooters, the cowgirl was praised for her talent and her beauty. She was the all-American girl, wholesome, outdoor-loving, and fearless. Announcers welcomed young women into the arena as equals of the cowboys. In 1913, the 101 Ranch had fifty woman on their staff, albeit not many, considering the entire troop of 1100 staff members and 600 elephants, camels, horses, buffalo, long-horned steers, oxen, mules, and ponies. Mark Twain believed the Wild West shows represented a truly American culture in which Americans especially should take pride. Another star performer was Lucille Mulhall. Reporters were impressed that she behaved like a woman. "Not only could she ride, rope and shoot but also play the piano, recite poetry, and make mayonnaise dressing."

In contrast to Annie Oakley, May Lillie did her trick-shooting from the back of a horse. In the mid-1880s, she claimed to be the only woman doing this stunt in a sidesaddle. *Circus World Museum.*

May Lillie and her husband, Wild West showman Pawnee Bill, c. 1890. *National Cowgirl Museum and Hall of Fame.*

BUFFALO BILL'S
WILD WEST
PAWNEE BILL'S
FAR EAST

PAWNEE BILL'S HISTORIC WILD WEST
AMERICA'S NATIONAL ENTERTAINMENT

PEERLESS EQUINE EDUCATOR, MISS MAY LILLIE,
IN HER UNEQUALLED EXHIBITION OF HIGH SCHOOL MENAGE, UNSURPASSED
CONTROL OF THOROUGHBREDS AND THEIR SUBMISSION TO WOMAN'S WILL.

(opposite) **Buffalo Bill and Pawnee Bill combined shows in 1909. This poster from the 1912 season presents an unusual contemporary-style sketch of a cowgirl with her pony. The show went bankrupt in 1912. Buffalo Bill Historical Center.**

May Lillie was the featured female rider with the Pawnee Bill Wild West Show. Conforming to Victorian standards, Lillie put her horses through their paces while riding sidesaddle. Circus World Museum.

May Lillie takes a bead with her Colt six-shooter in this publicity photo, c. 1908. Manns Collection.

Will Rogers supposedly coined the term "cowgirl" to describe Lucille Mulhall in 1899. Until that time, cowgirls were sometimes called "cow-boy girls." Born in 1885, Mulhall began her show career at age fourteen with her father Zack Mulhall's Wild West Show and later with the 101 Ranch Wild West Show. She could ride, wrestle a steer to the ground, and rope up to eight running horses at a time. Schmitt/Cayuse Collection.

A nineteen year-old Lucille Mulhall went to work for the Miller Brothers' 101 Ranch Wild West Show in the spring of 1905. By that time she was a recognized champion rodeo performer. She weighed less than a pair of stock saddles, but she could throw steers, bust broncs, and brand cattle. Young Mulhall perfected the stunt of roping up to eight galloping horses with a single loop. Mulhall grew up on a ranch roping and riding with her brothers and the cowhands. Her father noticed that she attracted plenty of compliments for her ranch skills. In 1899, Zach Mulhall organized a small Wild West show called "The Congress of Rough Riders and Ropers." Thirteen year-old Lucille Mulhall was the main headliner.

In 1899, the Mulhall family saw their first major publicity at the St. Louis Fair. Lucille Mulhall was part of the show, along with Will Rogers. She roped and tied steers in competition with the best of the cowboys. Her trick-riding act with her good horse Governor was always a hit. In succession, Governor did cakewalking, a quick step, and a side step, followed by a swing around an imaginary maypole with his front hoof bored into the turf. The horse went lame, played dead, rang a bell, took off his mistress's hat, walked on his knees, sat on his haunches, and crossed his forelegs! "Aren't you afraid your horse will slip and fall?" asked a Kansas newspaper reporter. "Oh I expect that," she replied. "I'm not afraid of getting hurt."

After Teddy Roosevelt saw Mulhall perform for his Rough Riders in 1900, he told Mulhall's father to take her on the road. Will Rogers called Mulhall (somewhat inaccurately) "America's first cowgirl." She started on the show circuit from her hometown to Madison Square Garden and attracted attention everywhere. Because the two families were friends, Mulhall also showed in the Miller Brothers' 101 Ranch Show with a number of female stars including Helen Gibson, Mabel Strickland, Flores LaDue, and Alice Lee. Other famous 101 Ranch cowgirl stars were Ruth Roach, Tillie Baldwin, and Mildred Douglas.

(below and opposite) **Juanita Parry wore this hand-made, beaded-fringed buckskin split riding skirt in Wild West shows only a few times. In 1917, she was killed after a fall during a performance. Buffalo Bill Historical Center.**

These stamps were souvenirs from the San Francisco Exposition of 1915. They featured several of the cowgirl stars, including the cowgirl twins, Juanita and Ethyle Parry from Oklahoma, who rode with the 101 Ranch and Buffalo Bill's Wild West Shows. Murphy Collection.

Martha Allen and the Parry sisters (below), who excelled in roping, picking up articles from the ground while riding at breakneck speeds, or pitching on a bucking bronc, pose with new saddles made by S.D. Myres of Sweetwater, Texas, c. 1910-1915. Murphey Collection.

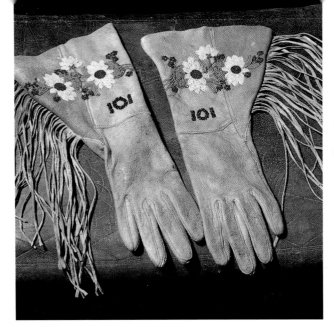

These buckskin riding gauntlets decorated in a floral beaded pattern must have been made for a female rider with the 101 Ranch Show in Oklahoma, c. 1915. Naramore Collection.

Fringed riding jacket and skirt worn by Ethyle Parry, c. 1915. Buffalo Bill Historical Center.

Cowgirls of the 101 Ranch Wild West Show rummage through a trunk for their costumes prior to an overseas performance. Because few companies made cowgirl outfits, many of the cowgirls designed and sewed their own. Murphey Collection.

(opposite) 101 Ranch Real Wild West Show featuring a Cow-Girl Bronco Buster, c. 1924. Circus World Museum.

70

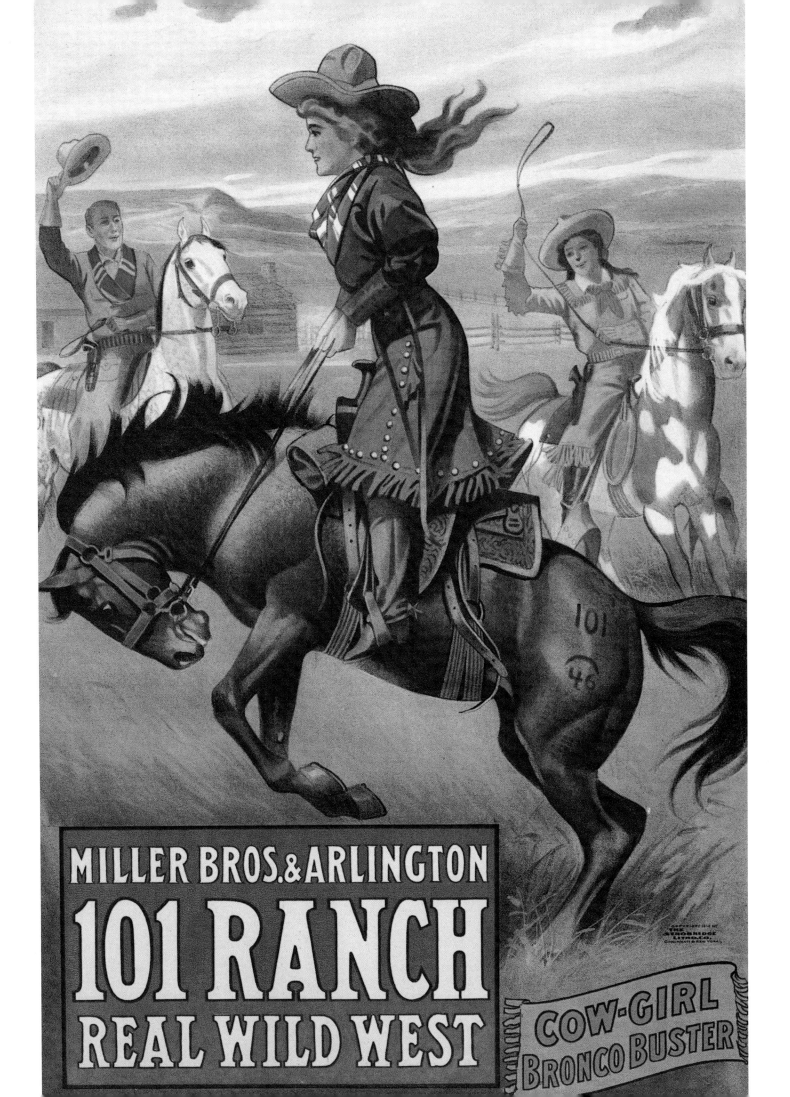

A group of cowgirl performers from the 101 Ranch Wild West Show pose along the pond at ranch headquarters in Bliss, Oklahoma, c. 1910. Cowboy Hall of Fame.

A young Wild West show cowgirl has left her sidesaddle for her husband's saddle in this unusual photo. Husband-and-wife teams were common in Wild West shows, many cowgirls having met their future spouses via the show circuit, c. 1900. Peck Collection.

(below) Many husband-and-wife teams performed in Wild West shows. Skilled horsemen and horsewomen had few opportunities to earn a living outside the arena, c. 1900. Peck Collection.

An illustration of a cowgirl on a spirited horse from a 101 Ranch Wild West Show poster, c. 1915-1920.

The Kemp Sisters' Wild West Show toured during the mid-1890s. It was one of the only shows of more than 120 that was operated by women. Circus World Museum.

(right) Cowgirls with early Wild West shows created and embellished their own costumes. This unknown performer sewed a row of buckskin fringe to the brim of her Stetson, c. 1900-1905. Murphy Collection.

(left) Adele Von Ohl Parker was a Wild West show performer with Buffalo Bill and also appeared in early silent movies as a cowgirl star. Denver Public Library, Western History.

(above) *Princess Wenona's Model 1873 lever action Winchester and a Model 1890 pump action .22 caliber Winchester are featured here with her gold-plated Smith & Wesson Double Action revolver and concha trophy belt. The gold buckle is inscribed: PRESENTED TO "WENONA" CHAMPION RIFLE SHOT OF THE WORLD BY DIRECTORS OF INDIAN CONGRESS, PAN AMERICAN EXPOSITION, AUGUST 17, 1901. Murphey Collection.*

Princess Wenona billed herself as the champion Indian girl rifle shot. Wenona (also known as Miss Lillian Smith) was actually a white woman. Sometimes called the "California Girl Champion Rifle Shot of the World," Wenona toured with both the Buffalo Bill and 101 Ranch Wild West Shows. Regardless of the costume she wore, Wenona was an expert shot and a skilled performer. Murphey Collection.

By masquerading as Indian Princess
Wenona, Lillian Smith distinguished
herself from other sharpshooters like
Annie Oakley and May Lillie.
Circus World Museum.

A Mexican cowgirl, featured on this
Wild West poster, added an element of
the exotic to the show, c. 1910-1920.
Holley Collection.

Later, Mulhall organized her own productions in which she continued to rope steers and trick-ride, often in competiton against the cowboys. In 1905 in Coffeeville, Kansas she defeated thirty-eight cowboys in a three-day steer roping contest; eight years later, again competing against cowboys in Winnipeg, Canada, she took second place and was given the title "Champion Lady Steer Roper of the World." Like many of the other cowgirls in Wild West shows, Mulhall also competed in rodeo. The remaining two Mulhall sisters were competent performers but never achieved the acclaim accorded to Lucille. Between 1880 and 1917, Wild West shows grew in size and number, but most of them ceased operation with the advent of World War I. A few continued into the 1940s and some still exist today. Alice Renner, an Iowa ranch girl who worked for Warner's Western Review in the 1930s, said that she performed for the money:

"People were getting three dollars a week for housework or for working in a store. You could get $25 a week working for a Wild West show," she said. Renner did a knife, rope, and whip act for the Western Review with Dakota Bob.

(above) *A Sioux beaded gun belt and holster, c. 1900. Indian performers who traveled with Wild West shows often made beaded items for the cowgirls. Deihl Collection.*

(left and below) *Annie Shaffer was a performer with Buffalo Bill's Wild West Show in the early 1900s. Shaffer carried a Colt Single Action revolver in her beaded holster and matching cartridge belt. Shown are Annie Shaffer's fringed skirt, matching vest, and beaded gun rig, which she wore in Buffalo Bill's Wild West Show. The skirt is decorated with the Indian symbol for good luck. Fisher Collection.*

Mrs. Pete Culbertson is pictured here in a split riding skirt with her cartridge belt and gun. Culbertson performed as a trick-shot with her husband in the Indian Pete Wild West Show, 1910-1915.

Leather cuffs were sometimes worn on the range to protect a westerner's shirt sleeves, but they were more popular as an added accessory in the Wild West shows. Neill Collection.

"MRS. PETE CULBERTSON" ENTIRE LIFE ON WESTERN PLAINS WITH INDIAN PETE'S WILD WEST

Wild West show girl Jane Bernoudy is at ease in her cowgirl outfit and "packing iron." University of Wyoming, American Heritage Center.

LuLu Parr, dressed in this extraordinary beaded outfit, rode buffalo, wild steer, and bucking horses for the Buffalo Bill Wild West Show, The Pawnee Bill-Buffalo Bill Combined Shows, and for the 101 Ranch Wild West Show, among others. Her costume, c. 1910-1915, is a combination of a traditional fringed leather split riding skirt with Indian beadwork. Her accessories, the high-top laced boots, gauntlets, arm bands, vest, and hatband, also feature Plains Indian-style beading. Buffalo Bill Memorial Museum.

The small size of these beaded Sioux spur straps indicates that they were probably used by a cowgirl. They were most certainly worn by a Wild West show performer, c. 1880. Schmitt/Cayuse Collection.

This cowgirl beaded belt features the rolling log image, a symbol of good luck among certain Native American tribes, c. 1905. Haller Collection.

"I used to let out the rope over my head and pop it 'till it roared. Then I'd take a matchbox off Dakota Bob's head." She started her Wild West career at eighteen and stayed in the business for four years. "We never had any trouble," she said. "We could get on at any fair." Their itinerary included Chicago, Salt Lake City, Billings, Winnipeg, and cities in Oregon and California.

"I enjoyed it," she concluded. "It went so fast, and it was so fun, I never had time to stop and think. We were on the go all the time."

Cowgirls in the Wild West shows enjoyed their stardom and played to the audience's fantasies. They wore beautiful costumes that accentuated their identity as heroines of the Plains. There was no question, however, that these women were proficient in what was considered traditionally a man's world.

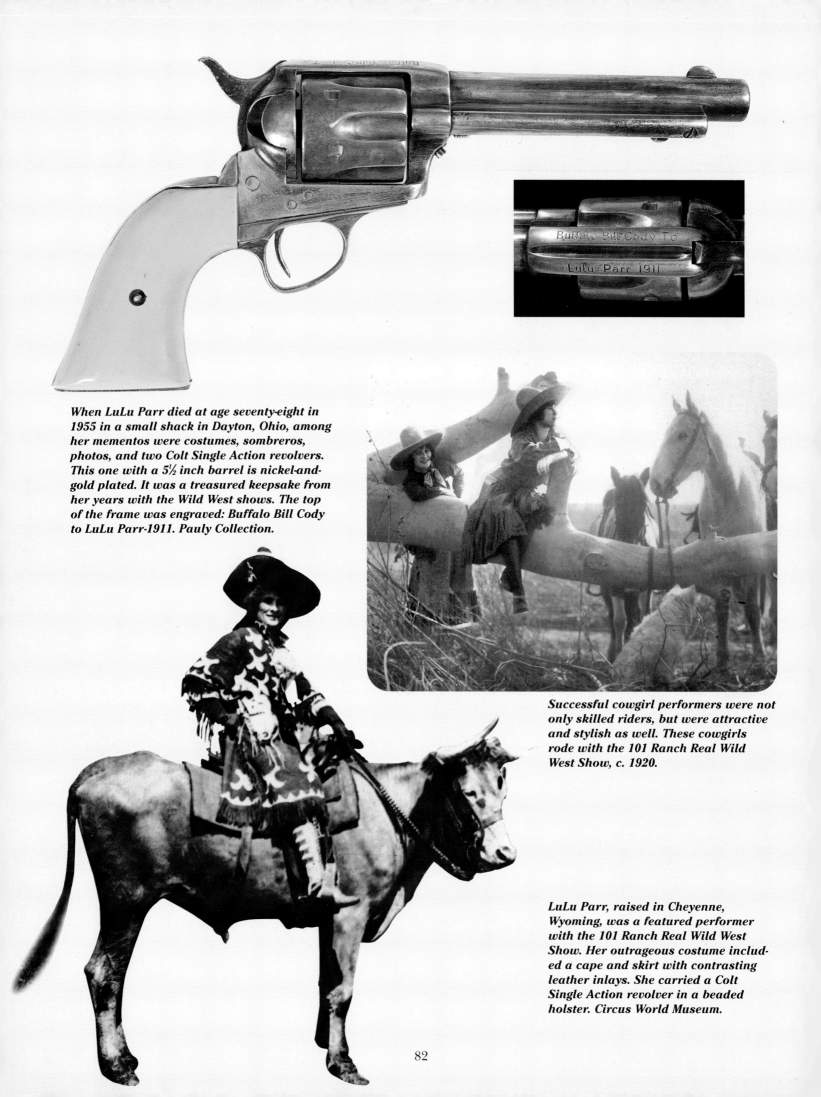

When LuLu Parr died at age seventy-eight in 1955 in a small shack in Dayton, Ohio, among her mementos were costumes, sombreros, photos, and two Colt Single Action revolvers. This one with a 5½ inch barrel is nickel-and-gold plated. It was a treasured keepsake from her years with the Wild West shows. The top of the frame was engraved: Buffalo Bill Cody to LuLu Parr-1911. Pauly Collection.

Successful cowgirl performers were not only skilled riders, but were attractive and stylish as well. These cowgirls rode with the 101 Ranch Real Wild West Show, c. 1920.

LuLu Parr, raised in Cheyenne, Wyoming, was a featured performer with the 101 Ranch Real Wild West Show. Her outrageous costume included a cape and skirt with contrasting leather inlays. She carried a Colt Single Action revolver in a beaded holster. Circus World Museum.

Women performed novelty acts, such as riding trick bulls, to attract large audiences. Opal Reger rides "Bobby," the "Educated Longhorn Steer." Cowboy Hall of Fame.

This poster for the 101 Ranch Real Wild West Show features LuLu Parr riding a buffalo. Circus World Museum.

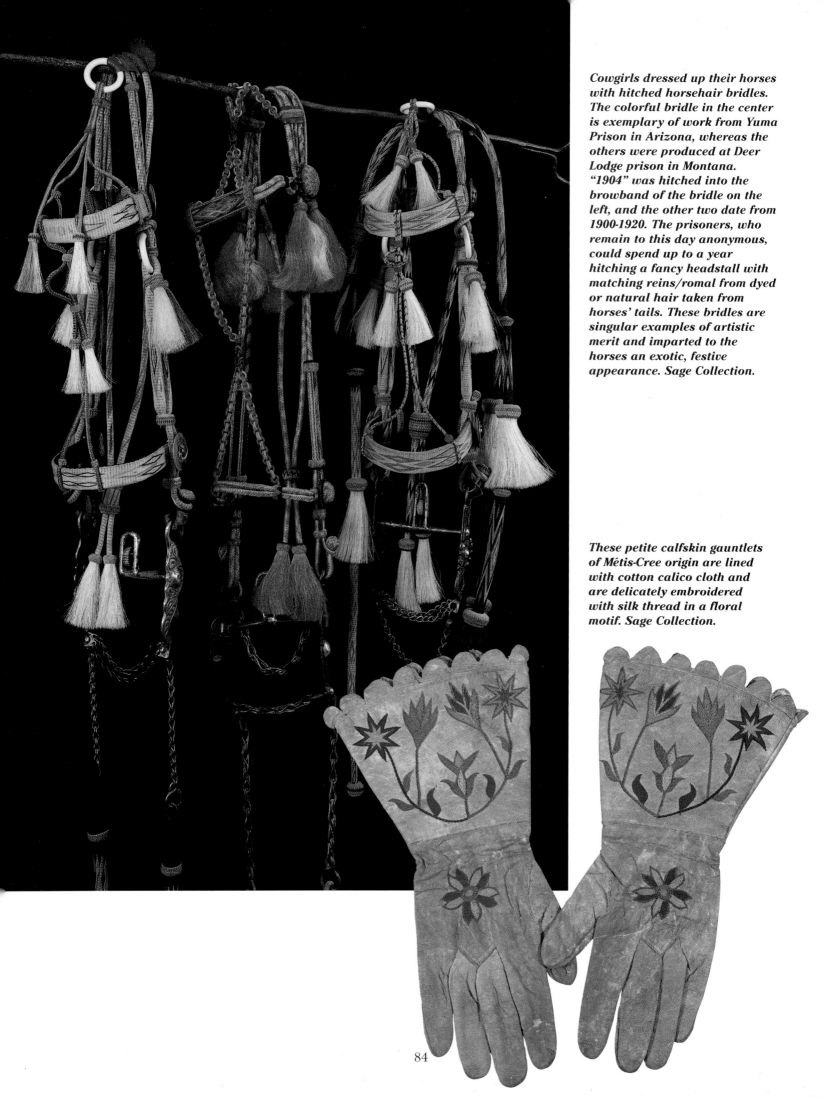

Cowgirls dressed up their horses with hitched horsehair bridles. The colorful bridle in the center is exemplary of work from Yuma Prison in Arizona, whereas the others were produced at Deer Lodge prison in Montana. "1904" was hitched into the browband of the bridle on the left, and the other two date from 1900-1920. The prisoners, who remain to this day anonymous, could spend up to a year hitching a fancy headstall with matching reins/romal from dyed or natural hair taken from horses' tails. These bridles are singular examples of artistic merit and imparted to the horses an exotic, festive appearance. Sage Collection.

These petite calfskin gauntlets of Métis-Cree origin are lined with cotton calico cloth and are delicately embroidered with silk thread in a floral motif. Sage Collection.

Wild West show cowgirl LuLu Parr appears in a fringed hair-on calfskin riding skirt and beaded vest with matching pictorial gauntlets. Her horse is fitted out in a fancy, prison-made hitched horsehair bridle and a saddle with white Angora serapes and dove-wing tapaderos. Wallgren Collection.

(Over leaf) *Although there were more cowboys than cowgirls in the Buffalo Bill and Pawnee Bill Wild West Shows, women often decorated the promotional posters. Buffalo Bill Memorial Museum.*

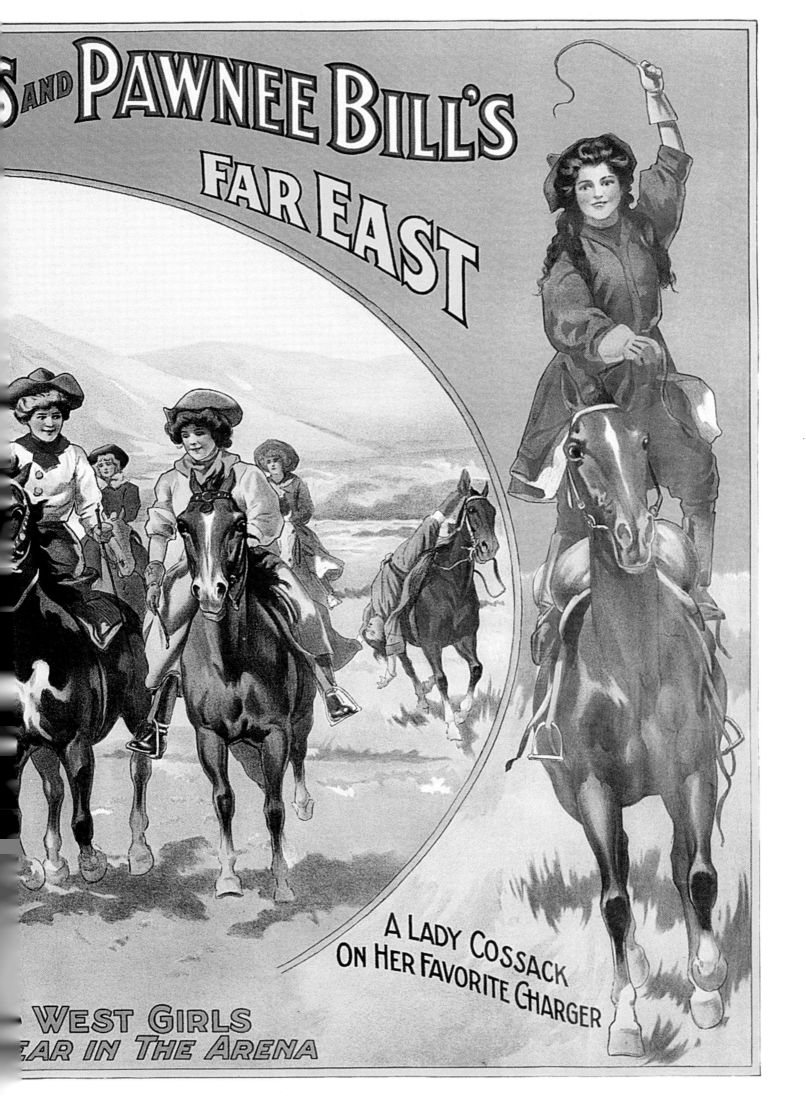

LET'ER BUCK

CHAPTER 3

In obedience to her parents' wishes, sixteen-year old Gene Krieg sat on a train bound for La Junta, Colorado to help her sister with her new baby. Krieg picked up a newspaper enroute and read about Frontier Days, the famous Cheyenne rodeo. Prize money up to $300 and trophies including a $75 cowboy hat and a silver belt buckle caught her eye, whereupon Krieg switched trains and headed to Cheyenne to compete for the title "Champion Cowgirl of the World." The baby diapers could wait. Krieg was going to ride a sunfishing bronc. The year was 1925.

A Colorado ranch girl, Krieg had broken wild horses with her brothers and sister since she was four. One year she rode down the streets of her home town, Holly, while standing on a galloping horse. At fifteen, she participated in the Watermelon Day parade in Rocky Ford, but aside from riding bucking calves and wild horses, she had no experience with rodeo broncs.

After finding a place to stay in Cheyenne, borrowing an outfit, and sending a telegram to her parents, Krieg flew out of the chute at Frontier Days on a pitching bronc named Blue Dog, a Powder River outlaw with a reputation for dumping his riders. With untied stirrup (most cowgirls hobbled or tied their stirrups to the cinch), Krieg stayed on the bucking horse, spurring fore and aft, just like the cowboys. Surprised by the excellent performance, the judges threw their hats in the air and pronounced Gene Krieg the "Champion Cowgirl of the World."

Krieg's new title was impressive, since she had competed against a group of a dozen talented, veteran cowgirls that included Ruth Roach, Mabel Strickland, Tad Lucas, Rose Smith, and Fox Hastings. Krieg's parents, who never

Waving a pair of American flags, this patriotic cowgirl circled the arena on her pony, c. 1915. Circus World Museum.

(opposite) Norwegian Tillie Baldwin was an accomplished rodeo star in the early 1900s. She roped, trick-rode, relay-raced, rode bucking horses, and was one of the few cowgirls who could wrestle a steer successfully. Helm Collection.

Colorado cowgirl Gene Krieg Creed traveled the world as a trick-rider in the twenties and thirties. Her career ended abruptly in 1941 before an audience at Madison Square Garden. Standing tall on her galloping horse Sheik, Creed prepared to fall backwards into a suicide drag, when her horse spooked at a fur coat tossed over the railing. Sheik stopped abruptly, upsetting Creed, who fell and dangled to the side. Someone tried to rescue Creed but succeeded only in spooking her horse further. The severe head injury resulting from this accident halted an illustrious career. National Cowgirl Museum and Hall of Fame.

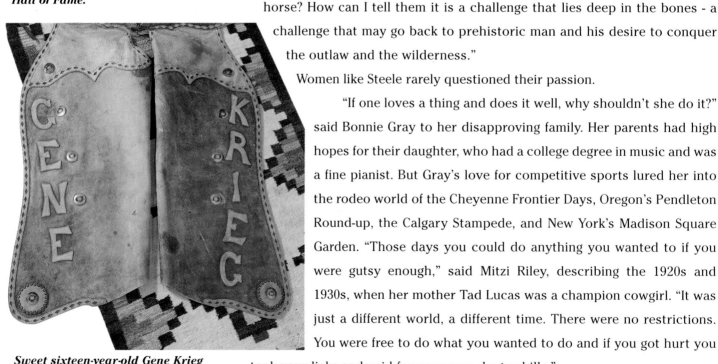

Sweet sixteen-year-old Gene Krieg spurred a bronc named Blue Dog at Cheyenne Frontier Days in 1925 to win the title "Champion Cowgirl of the World." Pictured here are Krieg's batwing-style rodeo chaps made by Hamley. National Cowgirl Museum and Hall of Fame.

received their daughter's telegram, were dumbfounded when their friends announced that Krieg had made the headlines in the Cheyenne paper: "She's a sweet champion - queen of hearts and hard horses."

The rodeo cowgirls of the 'teens and 'twenties were an unusual group of determined young ladies who chose to live a glamorous, unfettered, ambitious but dangerous life as competitors in many different events throughout America, Canada, Europe, Mexico, and Australia. They sought risk and thrived on adventure, competition, and the promise of fame and money. The lifestyle was difficult and dangerous, but most of these women would have refused to change their lives if given the opportunity.

"Sometimes it takes a lot of grit to do what you want to do, but I can't see how people can stand the monotony of doing work at which they are not happy," said Fanny Sperry Steele. "Rodeo teaches you that death is right around the corner, and the "now" is all you have, so make the most of it. It may be the old Anglo-Saxon creed, 'Eat, drink, and be merry for tomorrow you die' carried over into rodeo, but it fits. We live each day as if it's our last."

A rugged and wiry lady whose braids flew in the air over bucking horses from Calgary to New York City, Steele won numerous championships. Trying to explain her drive she once said: "How can I explain to dainty, delicate women what it is like to climb down into a rodeo chute onto the back of a wild horse? How can I tell them it is a challenge that lies deep in the bones - a challenge that may go back to prehistoric man and his desire to conquer the outlaw and the wilderness."

Women like Steele rarely questioned their passion.

"If one loves a thing and does it well, why shouldn't she do it?" said Bonnie Gray to her disapproving family. Her parents had high hopes for their daughter, who had a college degree in music and was a fine pianist. But Gray's love for competitive sports lured her into the rodeo world of the Cheyenne Frontier Days, Oregon's Pendleton Round-up, the Calgary Stampede, and New York's Madison Square Garden. "Those days you could do anything you wanted to if you were gutsy enough," said Mitzi Riley, describing the 1920s and 1930s, when her mother Tad Lucas was a champion cowgirl. "It was just a different world, a different time. There were no restrictions. You were free to do what you wanted to do and if you got hurt you took your licks and paid for your own doctor bills."

During a time when ladies still adhered to Victorian conventions, the rodeo cowgirls' zest for life awed thousands across the country. As widely recognized as Hollywood stars, these women rode bucking broncs in competitions with men; they roped and bulldogged steers, rode in relay

At the Winnipeg Stampede in 1913, champion cowgirl Tillie Baldwin wins a Roman riding race by outdistancing Johnny Mullens and A.J. Bryson. Glenbow Archives.

(above) Alice Sisty, who had a reputation for being wild, thrilled audiences by "Roman-riding" a pair of horses over a Cord convertible. Sisty worked for the Cremer shows during several seasons in the 1930s. High Noon Collection.

Riding her famous horse, King Tut, Bonnie Gray sails over a Cleveland auto (complete with passengers) at Cheyenne Frontier Days in 1925. Not only were these old-time open cars tall and dangerous to jump, but the heavy western saddle with cumbersome tapaderos made the jump even more difficult. Museum of Northwestern Colorado.

In a publicity shot taken by Ralph Doubleday, Ruth Roach feeds her pet pig. Roach was a flamboyant, accomplished cowgirl, who as Mitzi Riley said "hated to lose." She started trick-riding for the circus in 1914, and in 1917, on board Memphis Blues, Roach was the first cowgirl to ride a bucking horse at the Fort Worth rodeo. Schmitt/Cayuse Collection

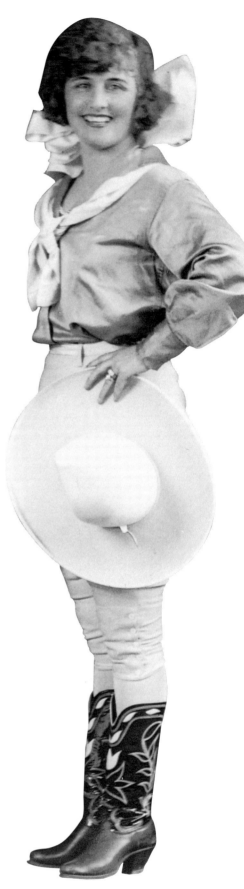

Ruth Roach models a 1930s cowgirl style. At this time, cowgirls wore this tailored look with tight-fitted pants and silk blouses. Hats were large and the boots more elaborate than they had been earlier in the century. National Cowboy Hall of Fame.

Eleanor Heacock performs an extremely dangerous stunt as she crosses under her horse's belly at a full gallop in Belle Fourche, South Dakota, 1934. An eastern debutante and graduate of Westover School in Middlebury, Connecticut, Heacock shocked her parents when she eloped with cowboy Walter Heacock and took a job with a Wild West show in Chile. Heacock continued to perform as a trick-rider and circus performer. She also ranched in Montana and in New Mexico, married three times, and was a painter and poet. National Cowboy Hall of Fame.

A collection of western jewelry owned by top cowgirls: Pauline Nesbett's charm bracelet, Norma Sanders's belt buckle, and Tad Lucas's silver compact and watch (both trophies) and a Navajo arm bracelet with thunderbird images, which she wore to camouflage her scar after her fall in 1933. National Cowgirl Museum and Hall of Fame.

TILLIE BALDWIN

Born in Norway as Mathilda Winger, Tillie Baldwin changed both her name and her career (formerly a hairdresser). The champion cowgirl created this hand-made bloomer outfit in 1913. Because clothing stores carried few cowgirl items at this time, cowgirls created their own costumes. Baldwin was well-known for her rodeo exploits at the Pendleton Round-up and Winnipeg Stampede. Glenbow Archives.

94

Seven-year-old Horace Day spins a small wedding ring atop Tillie Baldwin's shoulders while she is standing in the saddle during the Winnipeg Stampede in 1913. Glenbow Archives.

Most cowgirls who performed in rodeos from the mid-1890s through the early teens adopted costumes that were worn by the Wild West show performers. Tillie Baldwin is shown here with a seven-inch brim Stetson, fringed gauntlets, and a fringed riding skirt with contrasting leather overlays. She packs a "hog leg" on her hip. Low Collection.

95

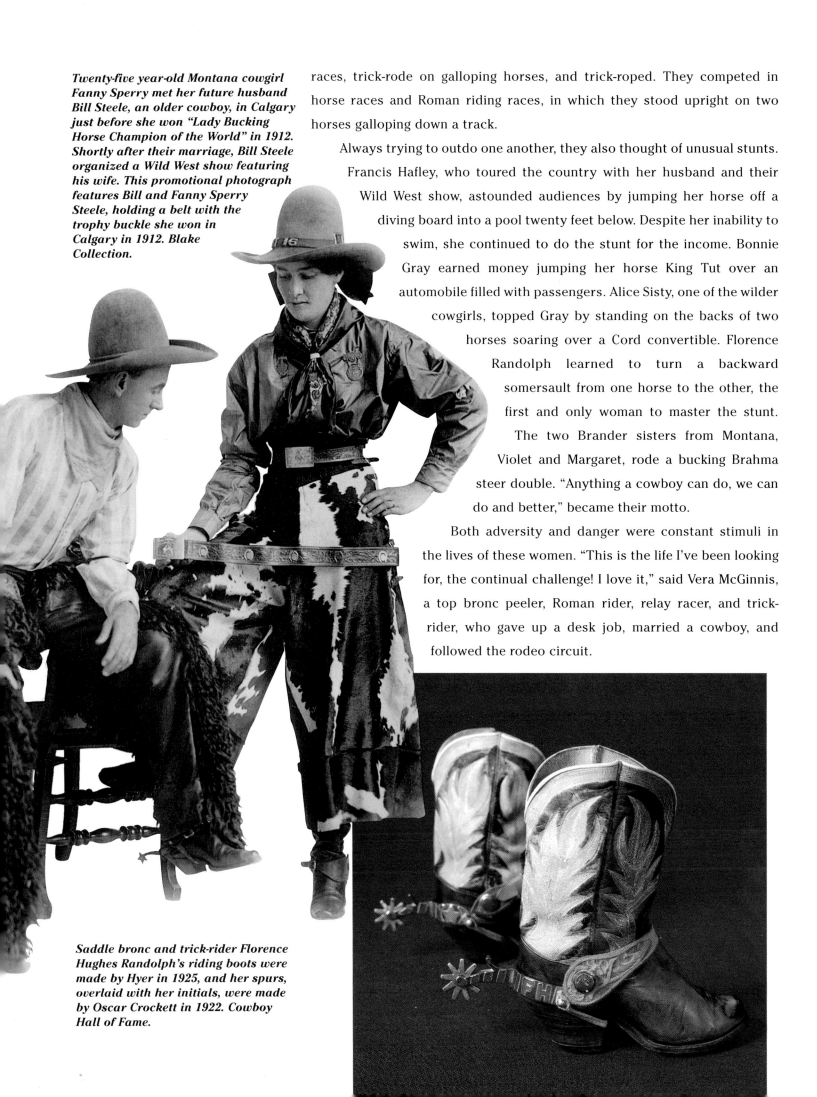

races, trick-rode on galloping horses, and trick-roped. They competed in horse races and Roman riding races, in which they stood upright on two horses galloping down a track.

Always trying to outdo one another, they also thought of unusual stunts. Francis Hafley, who toured the country with her husband and their Wild West show, astounded audiences by jumping her horse off a diving board into a pool twenty feet below. Despite her inability to swim, she continued to do the stunt for the income. Bonnie Gray earned money jumping her horse King Tut over an automobile filled with passengers. Alice Sisty, one of the wilder cowgirls, topped Gray by standing on the backs of two horses soaring over a Cord convertible. Florence Randolph learned to turn a backward somersault from one horse to the other, the first and only woman to master the stunt.

The two Brander sisters from Montana, Violet and Margaret, rode a bucking Brahma steer double. "Anything a cowboy can do, we can do and better," became their motto.

Both adversity and danger were constant stimuli in the lives of these women. "This is the life I've been looking for, the continual challenge! I love it," said Vera McGinnis, a top bronc peeler, Roman rider, relay racer, and trick-rider, who gave up a desk job, married a cowboy, and followed the rodeo circuit.

Saddle bronc and trick-rider Florence Hughes Randolph's riding boots were made by Hyer in 1925, and her spurs, overlaid with her initials, were made by Oscar Crockett in 1922. Cowboy Hall of Fame.

A Ralph Doubleday photograph features (left to right): Kitty Canutt, Prairie Rose Henderson, and Ruth Roach sharing a moment of comradery at the Pendleton Round-up. Canutt was the wife of the famous rodeo star and legendary Hollywood stuntman Yakima Canutt. Low Collection.

"Jad" Barnes

Colored pencil sketches by artist Charles Simpson during Tex Austin's rodeo in London in 1924. National Cowboy Hall of Fame.

(right) *Eventually, cowgirls were banned from entering competitive events. They went on to perform exhibitions such as trick-riding. This trick-riding saddle with the distinctive brass horn was made by W.L. Woods of Gainesville, Texas, c. 1915. Miller Collection.*

Charles P. Shipley of Kansas City, Missouri made this trick-riding saddle owned by Lucyle Richards. Richards called trick-riding "sissy stuff," but performed her tricks with flair. The two handles on the back of the saddle were for back work. A cowgirl held onto the handles, slid off the horse's tail, and touched the ground or she jumped from side to side off the horse's hips. The straps just below these handles held a cowgirl's feet as she did a tail drag— hung upside down over the horse's back end. Oxbow stirrups were often used on trick-riding saddles because they facilitated rapid entrance and exit, an important safety feature. The tall horn provided a sufficient two-hand grip for a variety of tricks. The straps below the horn were used to steady a rider when she did a slick stand—standing tall in the saddle. National Cowgirl Museum and Hall of Fame.

(opposite,top) **Polly Burson, who studied with Vera McGinnis, circles the arena doing top work, i.e. tricks performed on the saddle. Ground work included any tricks in which the cowgirl touched the ground, such as vaulting or somersaulting off the horse. Burson performed from 1938-1945. Polly Burson Collection.**

(right) *Bea Kirnan performs a crowd-pleasing trick-riding stunt at an early rodeo, c. 1915. Wyoming State Archives.*

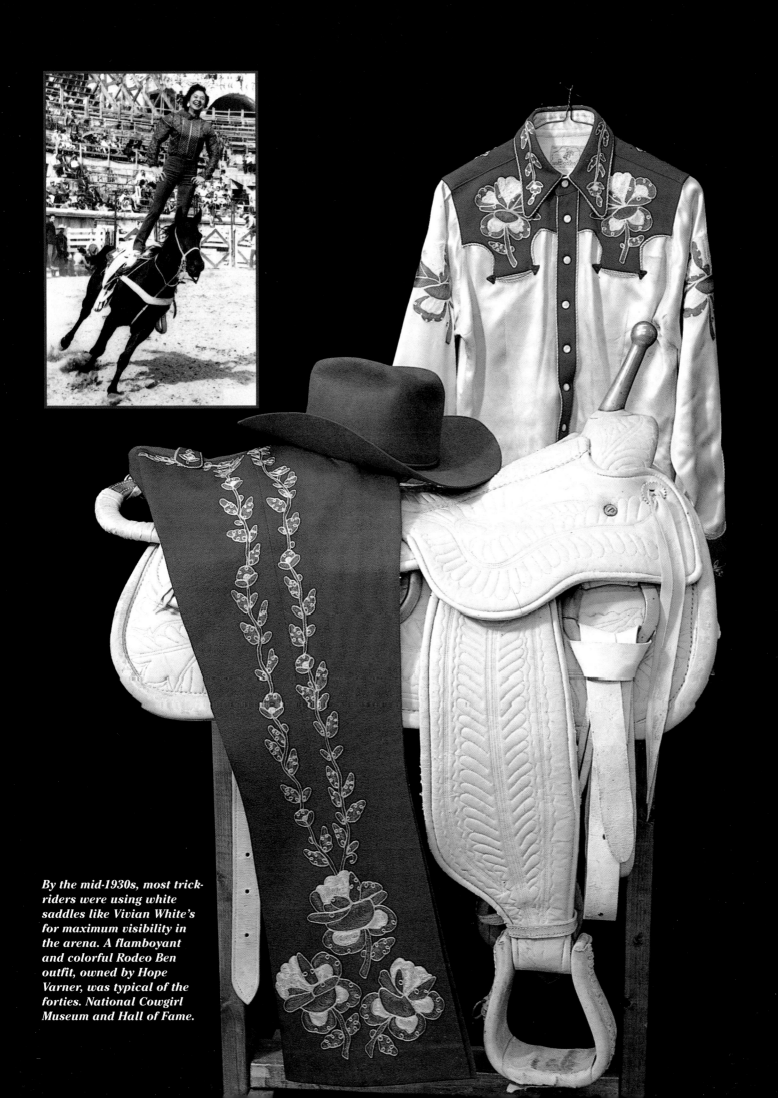

By the mid-1930s, most trick-riders were using white saddles like Vivian White's for maximum visibility in the arena. A flamboyant and colorful Rodeo Ben outfit, owned by Hope Varner, was typical of the forties. National Cowgirl Museum and Hall of Fame.

Felt contestants' numbers, which were worn on the arm, for bronc and trick-riding events, c. 1930s and 1940s. National Cowgirl Museum and Hall of Fame.

"Follering the rodeos or roundups is a hard way to make a livin', and at best it's a danged slim living," wrote Vera McGinnis in her book *Rodeo Road.* Ostensibly the excitement was worth the hardship and the cowgirls made enough money to get them to the next rodeo.

Early cowgirls accepted the dangers of the sport and exhibited tremendous stamina. In a trick-riding event in San Antonio in 1929, Florence Randolph fell off and was knocked unconscious. To the amazement of the audience, she opened her eyes, stepped off the stretcher, and completed her ride amid thunderous applause. In an interview afterwards she said simply, "It's all in the game."

Tad Lucas, a good bronc rider and talented trick-rider, almost ended her career in 1933 in a Chicago arena when she attempted to slide under the belly of a galloping horse. Unfortunately, she fell and was trampled. Her arm required six operations and several bone grafts. Lucas wore a cast for three years, but she was back on her horse in a year and performing tricks with one arm.

Like the others, Vi Brander thrived on the lifestyle.

"Rodeo riding is one of the most dangerous, nerve-wracking games there is, but I wouldn't trade one second of my arena life for all the rest of my life put together."

(opposite) **Rodeos were held throughout the world. The famous Pendleton Round-up in Oregon was one of the first rodeos to feature cowgirl contestants. This 1929 Pendleton poster features a cowgirl, unique for rodeo posters. Pokrifcsak Collection.**

1929 Pendleton **Round-up**

PENDLETON, OREGON

101

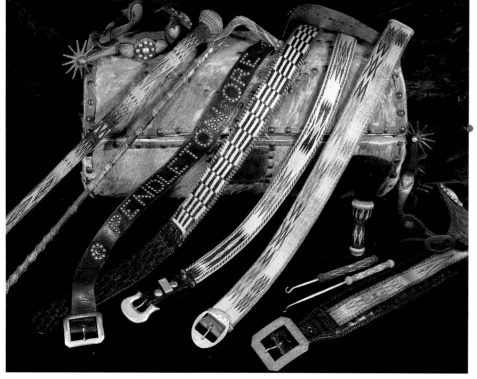

Cowgirl contestants in the Pendleton Round-up were promoted in a variety of competitive events, including saddle bronc riding. The cowgirls were unquestionably crowd-pleasers. *Low Collection.*

Cowgirls wore unique, stylish costumes, which set them apart from the cowboys. That they took great pride in their trappings is evident in this assortment of cowgirl belts, c. 1910-1930. *High Noon Collection.*

(above and below) **Rodeo cowgirl Helen Bonham was selected to be Miss Wyoming at Cheyenne Frontier Days' silver anniversary in 1917. "If it is for Wyoming, I'll do it gladly,"** she said. She was sent East to promote Frontier Days and Wyoming. For one publicity stunt she rode her horse in an elevator to the top of the McAlpin Hotel near New York City's Pennsylvania Station for the photograph that appeared on the cover of the "Mid-Week Pictorial," July 1, 1920. Schmitt/Cayuse Collection

Cowgirls liked to dress smart and carry fine luggage. These custom-made suitcases and hatbox are hand-carved leather. Reine Shelton's red hat, shirt, and belt, Norma Sanders's art deco-style purse, Hope Varner's leather purse, and Gene Krieg's bridle and white hat are also featured here. National Cowgirl Museum and Hall of Fame.

Lucyle Richards, bronc rider, trick-rider, and flying ace, joined the Cherokee Hammon's Wild West Show when she was thirteen. Tagged the "prettiest and best dressed cowgirl in America" by the press in 1934, Richards could also bulldog steers. She shot and killed one of her lovers. Prairie Rose Collection.

Regardless of how rugged the event was, cowgirls made a point of looking their best. Alice Greenough and her sister Margie Greenough apply their makeup before entering the arena. National Cowgirl Museum and Hall of Fame.

This compact with a bucking cowboy on the front is fabricated from pressed steer horn, c. 1930. Naramore Collection.

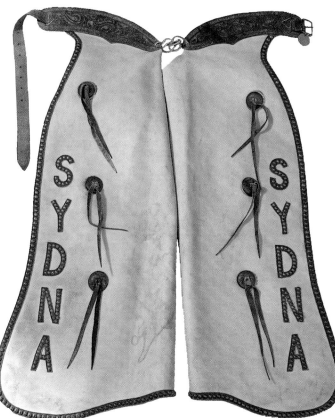

These batwing-style rodeo chaps belonged to Sydna Yokley Woodyard, a champion calf roper and trick-rider in the early 1940s and 1950s. She was one of the few calf ropers to perform at Madison Square Garden and the Boston Garden. She died tragically in 1959 when her horse panicked and kicked her to death in a horse trailer in Winslow, Arizona. National Cowgirl Museum and Hall of Fame.

The famous Buck Taylor Cowgirl Band, c. 1920. National Cowboy Hall of Fame.

This unusual rodeo pendant, c. 1916, features a cowgirl on a bucking horse. Lebel Collection.

Hoofs and Horns was a monthly publication for professional rodeo contestants, promoters, and performers. Rodeos by the mid-1930s featured glamorous rodeo queens as an important part of promotion for special events. Long Collection.

A formal portrait of the 1930s Pendleton Round-up Rodeo Queen and her court. (left to right): Virginia Sturgis, Evelyn Cresswell, Queen Lois McIntyre, Mildred Hansell, and Muriel Tulloch. Howdyshell Collection

This rodeo queen buckle was made by Eddy Hulbert, a famous bit and spur maker from the Big Horn, Wyoming area. Hulbert made scores of trophy buckles for rodeo events from 1930 to 1950. Lucille Mulhall was one of the first cowgirls to sport a silver buckle. Schmitt/Cayuse Collection.

The relay race was one of the early competitive events designed especially for cowgirls. These contestants were on the starting line at Cheyenne Frontier Days, c. 1898. Wyoming State Archives.

Champion rough-stock cowgirl Mildred Douglas rides a bucking steer. To her parents' chagrin, Douglas ran away from an eastern finishing school to work for the 101 Ranch in Bliss, Oklahoma. She rode in rodeo, performed in circuses, and worked briefly in Hollywood during her affair with Tom Mix. She was "World Champion Girl Bronc Rider" in 1917. Schmitt/Cayuse Collection.

Champion trick-rider Tillie Baldwin competed in bronc riding, relay-racing and trick-riding events. Realizing the importance of unrestricted movement in trick-riding contests, Baldwin wore bloomers which were not as cumbersome as the more traditional divided skirt, c. 1913. Helm Collection.

RODEO ROAD

The first cowgirls entered rodeo for the same reasons that motivated the men: for the excitement, the competition, and eventually, for the money. Because the first rodeos did not have special events for women, cowgirls demanded to compete against the cowboys.

Rodeo historian Milt Riske believes that Annie Shaffer, who rode a bucking horse in a Fort Smith, Arkansas rodeo in 1896, was one of the first cowgirl competitors. In 1897, Colorado ranch girl Bertha Kalpernik, later named Bertha Blancett, entered the wild horse race and the bucking contests in the men's program at Cheyenne Frontier Days. Kalpernik was talked into riding broncs when a cowboy refused to ride because the arena was too muddy.

Recalling Kalpernik's ride, Warren Richardson, chairman of the first Cheyenne Frontier Days committee, said, "One of the worst buckers I have ever seen but she stayed on him all the time. Part of the time he was up in the air on his hind feet; once he fell backward and the girl deftly slid to one side to mount him again as soon as he got up. She rode him to the finish."

In 1901, Frontier Days judges balked when Wyoming cowgirl Prairie Rose Henderson demanded to be allowed to enter the bucking bronc contest, an event open only to cowboys. Because the judges were unable to find any rules barring women from the competition, Henderson rode.

In 1904, Cheyenne opened their Frontier Days rodeo to women, and twenty-two year-old Kalpernik returned to compete. Her ride on Tombstone effectively stunned the audience (she was the only woman). Kalpernik went on to perform in the Pawnee Bill Wild West Show and two years later joined the Miller Brothers' 101 Ranch Wild West Show. At the 1911 Pendleton Round-up, she won a saddle in the cowgirl bucking bronc contest, and from 1911 to 1918 she was also All-Around Cowgirl. By this time, women in rodeo were recognized as athletes. They were also treated with respect. "I was always a lady," Kalpernik said. "They (the cowboys) treated me as such."

Guy Weadick, who produced the first Calgary Stampede in 1912, insisted on the participation of women, and all the leading cowgirls competed: Bertha Blancett, Dolly Mullins, Flores LaDue, Fanny Sperry, Lucille Mulhall, and Hazel Walker. Fanny Sperry, dressed in a split riding skirt and her characteristic bow-tied braids, won the title "Lady Bucking Horse Champion of the World." She took home $1,000, a saddle, and a belt buckle. Goldie Sinclair of Oklahoma was second and Bertha Blancett of Phoenix, Arizona earned third. In the fancy-

One of the earliest cowgirl competitors, Annie Shaffer rode a bucking horse at an Arkansas rodeo in 1896. Shaffer and her sister Lillian later became performers in the Buffalo Bill Wild West Show. Circus World Museum.

Flores LaDue, born Florence Benson, spins her rope on horseback at the first Calgary Stampede (1912), where she won the first world championships in trick and fancy-roping. Her husband, Guy Weadick, also a trick-roper, *helped to start the show. The couple met at the Chicago performance of the Wild West Show in 1906 and together were a well-known trick-roping pair. Glenbow Archives.*

Champion trick-roper, Jane Bernoudy, spins a wedding ring around her pony, c. 1918. Bernoudy toured with the C.B. Irwin Wild West Show and was one of cowboy star William S. Hart's many girlfriends. Wyoming State Archives.

roping contest, Flores LaDue placed first, Lucille Mulhall second, and Bertha Blancett third. Blancett also won the relay, and Dolly Mullins took home the trophy for the trick-riding.

The second Calgary Stampede in 1919 attracted Kitty Canutt, who was an expert trick, fancy, and Roman race-rider. Bertha Blancett competed against the men in relay racing and won the championship. Florence Hughes took on cowboys in the Roman race and also took first prize.

The rodeo season started in March at Fort Worth and ended in Boston in late November. Throughout the summer, cowgirls competed in the Cheyenne Frontier Days, Pendleton Round-up, Calgary Stampede, Salinas Rodeo, and Madison Square Garden. Some cowgirls went as far as London, Paris, Australia, Japan, Mexico, and/or Spain. Famous fancy-roper Flores LaDue once entered her address in a guest book as "The World."

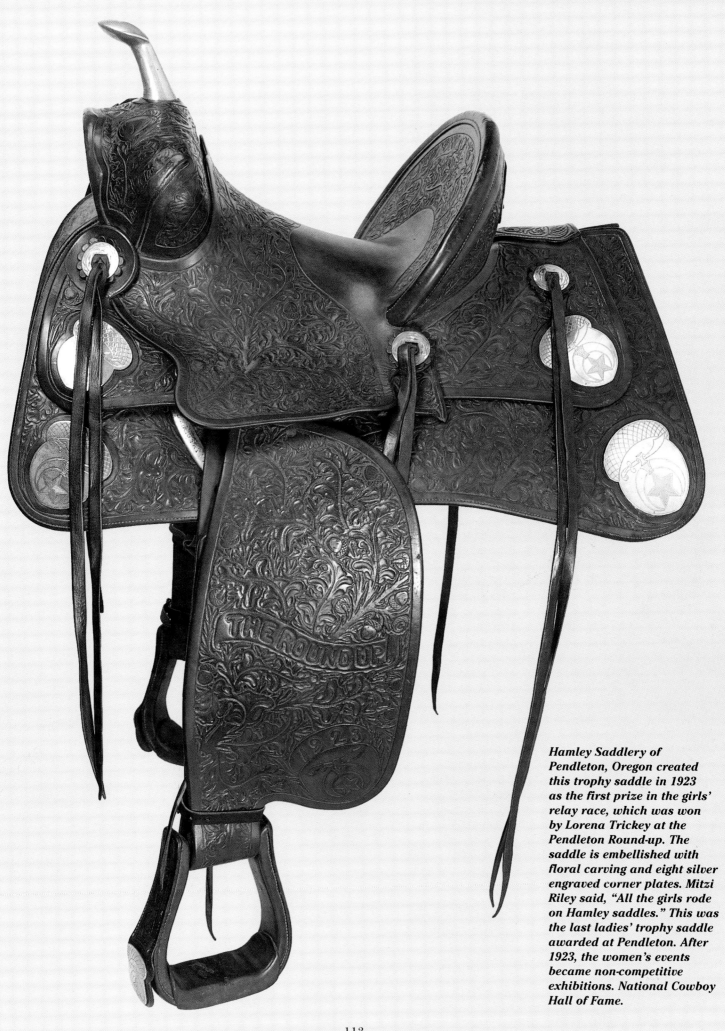

Hamley Saddlery of Pendleton, Oregon created this trophy saddle in 1923 as the first prize in the girls' relay race, which was won by Lorena Trickey at the Pendleton Round-up. The saddle is embellished with floral carving and eight silver engraved corner plates. Mitzi Riley said, "All the girls rode on Hamley saddles." This was the last ladies' trophy saddle awarded at Pendleton. After 1923, the women's events became non-competitive exhibitions. National Cowboy Hall of Fame.

114

(opposite) **In 1915, Bonnie McCarroll took a bad fall at the Pendleton Round-up. Fourteen years later at the same rodeo, McCarroll failed to extricate herself from her hobbled stirrups as she fell from a bronc. She died several days later of internal injuries. This accident hastened the demise of cowgirls' entering rough-stock competitions.**

(right) **O.J. Snyder Saddlery of Denver made this bronc-riding saddle for Bonnie McCarroll. The saddle incorporates a short, deep seat with a high cantle and a wide-swell fork for stability, a design known as a bear trap. The ring-style stirrups helped the cowgirl avoid entanglement when she fell or dismounted. National Cowboy Hall of Fame.**

Up in the air on the hurricane deck of a pony, these cowgirls loved to let 'er buck. (left to right): Pauline Nesbitt rides Two Step at the Tucson Rodeo, Tad Lucas flies across the arena in her woolly chaps, Dorothy Morrell spurs Skuball, and Mary Parks sits high in Kansas City on a bucking gray cayuse. National Cowboy Hall of Fame.

An unusual pen-and-ink drawing by Charles M. Russell of a cowgirl riding a bronc. Russell preferred painting cowboys. Montana Historical Society.

The most prestigious and valuable trophy made for cowgirl rodeo contestants was commissioned by Metro Goldwyn Mayer Studios in 1927 at a cost of $10,000. The trophy honored the champion cowgirl at the Madison Square Garden World Series Rodeo. The coveted trophy was won by Florence Randolph in 1927. Tad Lucas became the permanent holder of the MGM trophy after three consecutive championships in 1928, 1929, and 1930. National Cowboy Hall of Fame.

By the 1920s rodeos regularly featured three cowgirl events: ladies' bronc riding, trick-riding, and a cowgirl relay race. Some rodeos also offered bull riding, bulldogging, and Roman racing. Championships were based on points, but the contestants made money when they won. "We were on our own, no salaries, no expenses guaranteed, no nothing - except the love of our work sandwiched between plain ego and guts," wrote Vera McGinnis.

In the bucking event, rodeos usually had two strings of horses: the showier broncs for the cowgirls and the more fractious ones for the cowboys, but in reality the cowgirls rode their share of rank animals. Cowgirls were required to stay on for eight seconds and could ride with two reins, unlike the cowboys, who had to ride one-handed for ten seconds. Women were also invited to ride with their stirrups tied together (hobbled), a misleading advantage given the danger of this type of restraint. Some veteran cowgirls, like Fanny Sperry and Bertha Blancett, never hobbled their stirrups. They were proud of their accomplishments—Florence Randolph claimed to have won more bronc riding contests than any other girl in the world.

The rodeo road was grueling. Fanny Sperry's toughest rodeo was at the Milwaukee Fair. "I rode forty-two bucking broncs in one week. We put on eleven shows a day. I rode in six bucking events every day for a solid week, but I loved

These diminutive cowgirl riding boots with floral inlay and kangaroo vamps over high underslung heels were made by Hyer Boot Co. in 1928 for rodeo champion Tad Lucas. McChesney Bit and Spur Co. made the spurs, which are silver-mounted with drop shanks and chap guards. The auxiliary heel straps add stability when spurring a horse out of the chute. National Cowboy Hall of Fame.

every minute of it."

Trick/fancy riding was a competitive event among the women. At a full gallop, they performed stunts such as standing, dragging, vaulting, or passing under the horse's belly. The cowgirls were judged on originality, gracefulness, and skill, as well as on the difficulty of the stunt. They were always trying to outdo each other. Tad Lucas was a tough cowgirl to beat. She won the women's trick-riding contest at Madison Square Garden eight times during the 1920s and 1930s.

Relay racing was another popular cowgirl event. Each cowgirl had three horses, each of which would circle the track once. The best relay racers perfected the flying change, i.e., leaping through the air from one horse to the next.

Throughout the late 'teens into the 1930s, the rodeo circuit was a tightly-knit group. The men and women were generally supportive of each other. Most of the time they traveled by train, accompanied by the stock and their personal gear, their trunks packed with clothes and necessary items like spurs and hats. "We would play cards from here to New York," Texas champion Tad Lucas said. "The

Awarded by New York's McAlpin Hotel at the Cheyenne Frontier Days Rodeo, this prestigious cowgirl trophy was a relief cast bronze plaque finished in gold and enamel. Lorena Trickey won the trophy in 1920 for the Cowgirl Relay Race. National Cowboy Hall of Fame.

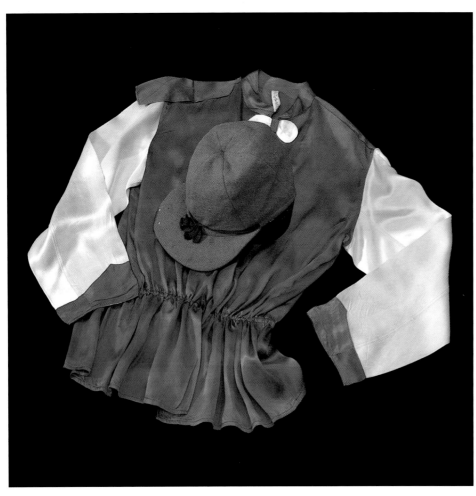

Relay racers wore silk riding costumes. The hat belonged to Reine Shelton, and the blue shirt to Anna Lee Aldred of Pueblo, Colorado, who competed in the 1930s and 1940s. Aldred was the first woman to receive her jockey's license in 1939. National Cowgirl Museum and Hall of Fame.

A Doubleday photograph of 1922 Pendleton Round-up relay race winners. (left to right): Lorena Trickey, Vera McGinnis, Mabel Strickland, and Donna Glover. National Cowgirl Museum and Hall of Fame.

In a trademark pose, Mabel Strickland ropes a steer at the Pendleton Round-up in 1922. A Ralph Doubleday photograph, National Cowgirl Museum and Hall of Fame.

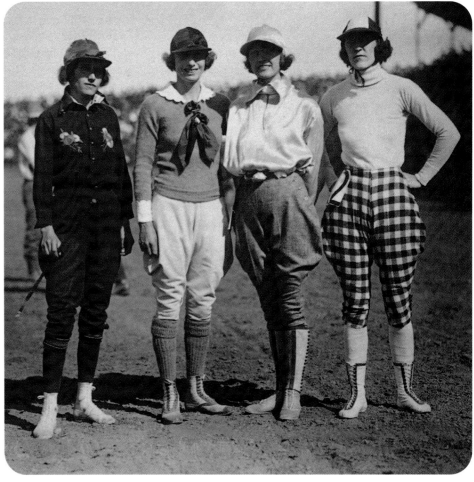

girls would play together, just penny ante and dimes. We never bet over a quarter, I'm sure. 'Course the cowboys played for big money." Some women took the time to repair and sew new costumes.

For shorter distances people traveled by car and trailer, or they simply rode. The Brander sisters, who stayed closer to home, traveled in the Northern Rockies by horse and slept in their bedrolls on haystacks.

In May of 1924, John Tex Austin took a group with many of the top female performers to Europe. The show was well-received and the performers were wined and dined by royalty. As one reporter noted, "At dances white tails mixed with chaps and satin shirts and boots. Ruth Roach convinced the English society to dance to a ragtime band and the cowboys and cowgirls amused their hosts with a square dance."

Sadly, the golden years for the cowgirl, when she competed in bucking events, trick-riding, and races, and was as famous as a Hollywood star, was destined to end. A combination of factors was responsible for this reversal. There were a few fatal accidents that might have discouraged rodeos from the inclusion of women's events. Bonnie McCarroll took a fatal fall at the Pendleton Round-up

Five distinctive cowgirls at the 1926 Pendleton Round-up display various versions of oversized hats, English breeches, and flashy ponies. Cowgirls liked paint horses because they stood out in the arena. Note the range of bridles from silver to Indian-style. Lebel Collection.

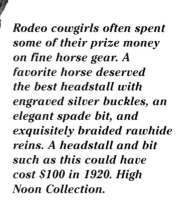

Rodeo cowgirls often spent some of their prize money on fine horse gear. A favorite horse deserved the best headstall with engraved silver buckles, an elegant spade bit, and exquisitely braided rawhide reins. A headstall and bit such as this could have cost $100 in 1920. High Noon Collection.

Eloise Fox Hastings's cowgirl career began in 1924 with a bulldogging exhibition at the Houston Stock Show. Hastings from Sacramento, California, went on to ride rough stock and was known to remark before she sprinted out of a chute: "If I can just get my fanny out of the saddle and my feet planted, there's not a steer that can last against me." Hastings took her own life in Phoenix, Arizona. National Cowboy Hall of Fame.

Fox Hastings, one of the few women to wrestle steers in the arena, ran away from home at the age of fourteen to be a cowgirl with the Irwin Brothers' Wild West Show, with which she performed trick-riding and bronc riding.

Cowgirl stars after World War I.: (left to right): Kitty Canutt, Ruth Roach, Mabel Strickland, Florence Hughes, Bea Kirnan, and Prairie Rose Henderson. Wyoming State Archives.

Mabel Strickland ties a steer. Strickland, also a trick-rider, relay-racer, and bronc-rider, was called by newspapers "The Lovely Lady of Rodeo." University of Wyoming, American Heritage Center.

This fancy eighteen-pound cowgirl skirt, c. 1920, is heavily decorated with heart-shaped conchas. Because of the skirt's weight, the original owner was probably a sharpshooter, as opposed to a bronc- or trick-rider. The skirt is featured with a spotted, bronc-buster belt. Smith Collection.

Cowgirls on rodeo posters were shown in popular events that included trick-roping, steer-riding, and trick-riding. Pokrifcsak Collection.

in 1929. Besieged with bad publicity, the Round-up eliminated women's bronc riding. Other rodeos followed suit. The Rodeo Association was unresponsive to women and ignored their pleas to be included. Instead, the Association invoked more regulations that limited competitions for cowgirls.

The Great Depression of 1929 also took a toll on rodeos. The Rodeo Association could no longer afford to pay for stock for both men and women; hence, the latter group was eliminated. Predictably, there were some hard feelings. "Money's the real reason," wrote cowgirl and historian Reba Perry Blakely. "I got this right out of the horse's mouth then in 1930. They said they wanted to keep the cowgirls out and put all the money into men's events. The cowboys told me if the rodeo association was going to pay any money, they wanted it."

In 1931, a rodeo producer in Stamford, Texas sponsored contests to add allure and boost attendance. Women were awarded prizes for horsemanship and an attractive horse, as beauty was considered more important than skill.

122

A cowgirl raises her arm for balance on a bucking bronc. Wyoming State Archives.

Decoration of this spotted bronc-buster belt with a heart indicates that it was made for a cowgirl. Smith Collection.

This cowgirl is wearing a bronc-buster belt, used to support internal organs, especially the kidneys. Many a cowgirl and cowboy would urinate blood after getting off a hard bucker.

From 1908 to 1914, Mamie Frances Hafley, shown at right and below, made over 626 jumps on her diving horse. She ended up breaking her nose twice, and her ankle and ribs once. The horse was led up a steep wooden ramp to approximately thirty-five feet above a large, eight-foot deep wooden tank. The horse would slide down a steep chute positioned over the center of the water. It was a dangerous stunt but a true crowd-pleaser. Eunice Winkless of Pueblo, Colorado was one of the first women to attempt this trick in 1905. National Cowgirl Museum and Hall of Fame.

These girls were the first of the rodeo queens, the glamorous figures in today's rodeo arenas. Their introduction into rodeo, formerly a stage for skill and daring, did much to kill the Golden Age of the Cowgirl. In the 1940s, although his trick-riders were the best of their time, Gene Autry helped promote the image of the pretty, helpless cowgirl in the rodeo with his Flying A Rodeo Company. This rodeo was entirely Hollywood-style, and the glamour girls took positions on the periphery. Their image as a counterfoil for the cowboy's various attributes was mirrored in the popular films of the decade.

Lady bronc riding was discontinued as a contest after 1941, the last year Madison Square Garden featured this event. Relay racing was waning, a few women bulldogged, and trick-riding continued as a contract act. In 1942 barrel racing was introduced into the professional rodeo circuit. Sponsors or glamour girls from the western states rode in the grand entry at Madison Square Garden and competed as barrel racers.

After World War II, a small group of women organized the Woman's Professional Rodeo Association, formerly the Girls' Rodeo Association, the oldest organization of female professional athletes in America and the only one controlled and managed entirely by women. The organization, which has over two thousand members, has succeeded in reinstating female contests that include bareback bronc riding, bull riding, ribbon roping, breakaway roping (in which the calf is roped but not tied), steer undecorating, and barrel racing. Lynn "Jonnie" Jonckowski, one of the few women today still competing in rough-stock events, was the 1986 and 1988 World Champion Bull Rider from Montana. "It didn't take guts for me to ride bulls," she said. "It took guts to buck the people who didn't want me to do it." With prize money up to a million dollars, rodeo for women has become a serious athletic event. Today's cowgirl competitors are assuredly not the celebrities epitomized by Prairie Rose Henderson and her colleagues, dressed in silk and chiffon, but they are nevertheless riding high on the hurricane deck of a bucking horse and earning a living with the courage, skill, and determination that characterized the old-time cowgirl. And, they are still every bit as feminine as their predecessors. As bull and bronc rider Jan Edmonson says, "My daddy always told me, 'You can be tough, but when you start being rough, you're through'." Perhaps champion barrel racer and roper Sammy Thurman sums up most accurately the joy of being a cowgirl in both the nineteenth and twentieth centuries. "You're your own boss and you go where you want to go," she said. "But you have to be a good hand."

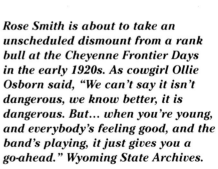

Rose Smith is about to take an unscheduled dismount from a rank bull at the Cheyenne Frontier Days in the early 1920s. As cowgirl Ollie Osborn said, "We can't say it isn't dangerous, we know better, it is dangerous. But... when you're young, and everybody's feeling good, and the band's playing, it just gives you a go-ahead." Wyoming State Archives.

Grace White takes a "bad spill" at the Arkansas-Oklahoma Rodeo. Her sister Vivian White, also a bronc rider, stretches out a helping hand. Wyoming State Archives.

Jane Bernoudy spins a wedding ring over her head. She is wearing a split riding skirt, the most popular riding costume from about 1900-1915. National Cowgirl Museum and Hall of Fame.

Vera McGinnis was the first cowgirl to wear pants in the arena. She was photographed in London in 1924 in this satin bolero and trousers. One of the more glamorous and stylish cowgirls, McGinnis set a standard that others followed. National Cowgirl Museum and Hall of Fame.

The cowgirls wanted to look different from each other; they enjoyed being conspicuous. One of the first cowgirls to sew outrageous colorful outfits was redheaded Prairie Rose Henderson, born in 1875 in Bristol, Ohio. Here she is at Cheyenne Frontier Days wearing a home-made outfit: a sequined vest and pantaloons with sequined pockets. Schmitt/Cayuse Collection.

RODEO STYLE

Despite the broken bones and the long hours on the road, many of the early cowgirls admitted that rodeo in the 'teens and 1920s was glamorous. When asked what motivated her to live such a hard life, Bonnie Gray answered: "Oh honey, I loved it. I was tops in this and tops in that. I just loved being tops!" Cowgirls thrived on the attention and they embraced their stardom by dressing smart.

The cowgirl was once said to be "all westerned up in her colorful rags." Since there was nothing suitable to buy *via* mail-order, most competitors made their own costumes. In the late nineteenth century, cowgirls like Annie Oakley and Lucille Mulhall wore long split riding skirts. As these women soon discovered, long skirts were impractical and in some cases were extremely dangerous. Cowgirls thus started making functional changes but tried to keep their costumes feminine.

To lessen the danger of entanglement between the fabric and the stirrups, cowgirls first shortened their skirts. They made leather, canvas, or corduroy split riding skirts that ended just below the knees. Some of these skirts contained a middle panel which concealed the reality that these outfits were pants, especially important when the women were aground. Tall boots and bloomers covered any exposed leg area.

When Vera McGinnis started riding in rodeos in 1912, she wore a corset, because all women were expected to wear them. After her first relay, McGinnis tossed the corset. "I wished wholeheartedly that my long corset was in Hades," she said. McGinnis went on to design many outfits that had an enormous influence on the evolution of cowgirl attire. One of the first outfits McGinnis made for herself was a corduroy riding skirt for trick-riding. She went on to make even fancier split skirts.

"The cowgirls all wore heavily-fringed leather skirts and bolero jackets," McGinnis said. "The fanciest outfits were weighed down with beautiful Indian beadwork. I'd rather have had one of those costumes than a diamond tiara."

One of the most coveted outfits was the one worn by Mildred Douglas, who rode in rodeos and Wild West shows from 1916-1926 and was at one time

(above) **Prairie Rose Henderson was a skilled rodeo competitor in the first two decades of the twentieth century. In 1901, she demanded to be allowed to ride at Cheyenne Frontier Days. Because she was able to prove that there were no rules barring women from the event, the judges allowed her to compete. Henderson married more than five times, and finally retired to** **the Hadsell ranch near Rawlins, Wyoming with her husband Charles Coleman, a cattle rustler. One afternoon in 1932, authorities arrived to take him to jail. Henderson stayed on the ranch. Several weeks later Coleman returned to find his wife missing. On July 17, 1939, a Mexican sheepherder that was fighting a fire in the area found Henderson's body.** **Henderson's brother as well as her husband identified her by her ring, a bridle, her grain bucket, and articles of clothing. Henderson was apparently trying to catch a horse, but froze to death in a snowstorm. Her death certificate establishes her death at the age of fifty-eight in February, 1933 and her occupation: housewife. Schmitt/Cayuse Collection.**

127

This collection of cowgirl rodeo scarves dates from 1900 to 1930. Bucking horses were one of the most popular decorations. Many rodeos created custom scarves for their special events.

128

Tom Mix's lover. Her outfit was a short, split leather riding skirt, embellished with silver conchas and matched with a fringed bolero.

McGinnis and the other cowgirls soon discovered that even the short skirts were too cumbersome and restrictive. ". . . we put elastic in the skirt hems and let them blouse over. That at least kept them down," McGinnis said. These were the first bloomers. Soon cowgirls were sewing billowy satin pants which they wore with silk stockings, matching hair ribbons, brightly-colored scarves and sashes, and tall boots and hats. Large triangular scarves hung to a point in back and were tied in a knot in the front. In the 1920s-1930s they also wore armbands, which kept their puffed sleeves from interfering with their riding. For safety reasons, trick-riders even tossed their cowboy boots. "We wore sneakers - rubber soled tennis shoes - which were safer and easier for jumping off and on horses," McGinnis said.

The leather-fringed skirts and high-topped boots continued to supplement the bloomers in the arena until the mid/late 1920s and into the 1930s, when jodhpurs and breeches became popular. These English riding trousers bloused at the hip and buttoned tightly around the calf.

During this period of transition, cowgirls designed clothes to suit their lifestyle, in part because cowgirl outfits were difficult to find in stores. In 1919, Florence Randolph said that her goal was to make sixteen new outfits a year — it was her winter activity. Sadly, one winter McGinnis made a trunkful of clothes that ended up in the Snake River near Jackson Hole. She was totally discouraged and was forced to compete in only the few outfits that survived.

Cowgirls took the opportunity to make personal statements with outrageous outfits. Because many of the girls performed in Wild West shows, their colorful costumes carried over into rodeo. Brilliant scarves hung from their necks, and ribbons decorated their pigtails. Prairie Rose Henderson designed some of the most memorable outfits. In 1918, Henderson wore bloomers under a short skirt made of ostrich feathers. Tad Lucas remembers seeing this extraordinary outfit at a rodeo in Gordon, Nebraska. The skirt was made of colorful ribbons and sequins and was accompanied by a matching bolero jacket. Her prominent teeth and corkscrew curls were complimented by a heart headstall, the epitome of style.

"Prairie Rose was the queen of fashion in her chiffon, sequins and fur," wrote McGinnis about another outfit. She wore "bloomers with a long matching overblouse trimmed in chiffon, sequins, and a wide band of marabou feathers. With this of course she wore matching stockings, a widebrimmed tall crowned western hat, boots, and spurs."

Other girls had their trademarks. Bernice Taylor, known in the East as the Gardenia Lady, always wore the white flower in her hair during her

The fashionable cowgirl of the 1920s might be wearing lace-up riding boots with spurs mounted on the heels, a fine leather split riding skirt, a silk bandana, and a high-crown, wide-brimmed Stetson with a braided and stitched horsehair hatband. *Mackin Collection.*

This cowgirl's split riding skirt is made of fringed cowhide and is heavily decorated with nickel-plated, heart-shaped conchas. *Schmitt/Cayuse Collection.*

131

Cowgirl boots inlaid with an intricate butterfly pattern, c. 1930, with the owner's name LaNelle stitched into the tops. Sage Collection.

Mabel Strickland was one of the foremost cowgirl rodeo contestants from the mid-teens through the early 1930s. Here she shows off a pair of boots reportedly fashioned for her by her father, a shoemaker and obviously talented bootmaker. National Cowboy Hall of Fame.

Early boots were stitched in decorative patterns to add strength and rigidity. Cowgirls were not content with plain black boots worn by men. To meet their demands, makers added floral colored inlays. This unmarked pair has inlaid flowers and underslung heels, c. 1905-1920. Sage Collection.

(below left) Pauline Nesbitt, a rodeo star of the 1920s, shows off a new pair of fancy inlaid boots. National Cowboy Hall of Fame.

These custom boots by C.P. Shipley of Kansas City, Missouri, with steer heads were made for rodeo star Louise Lambert in 1925. Similar to their regard for hats, cowgirls took pride in their boots as a badge of office. Neill Collection.

133

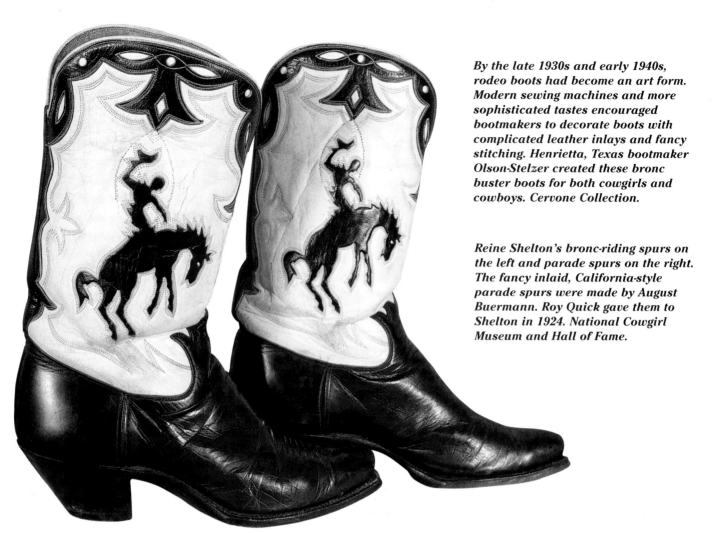

By the late 1930s and early 1940s, rodeo boots had become an art form. Modern sewing machines and more sophisticated tastes encouraged bootmakers to decorate boots with complicated leather inlays and fancy stitching. Henrietta, Texas bootmaker Olson-Stelzer created these bronc buster boots for both cowgirls and cowboys. Cervone Collection.

Reine Shelton's bronc-riding spurs on the left and parade spurs on the right. The fancy inlaid, California-style parade spurs were made by August Buermann. Roy Quick gave them to Shelton in 1924. National Cowgirl Museum and Hall of Fame.

Cowgirl Thena Mae Farr of Seymour, Texas had her boots and spurs decorated with her nickname "Tuffy." Farr rode broncs, barrel-raced, and was the president of the Girls' Rodeo Association in 1948. National Cowgirl Museum and Hall of Fame.

The original caption on this Doubleday photograph read "Bronc Riders 'and good ones.'" Not only were these women distinguished by their skills, but their large hats made them stand out in a crowd. Cowgirls typically wore the larger-brimmed cowboy hats beginning in 1905. National Cowgirl Museum and Hall of Fame.

Most hats were unisex. This unusual hat was made for cowgirls. A photo of Florence Hughes Randolph stitched into the lining was a product endorsement for this hat company, c. 1926. Holley Collection.

These fine Stetsons have crowns that measure seven or eight inches in height, with six-inch brims. The hats have pencil-rolled edges with ribbon binding. The crowns are variations of the Carlsbad crease, one of the most popular styles from 1915-1930. Robertson Collection.

No hat held ten gallons of anything, but rodeo star Tad Lucas did put her light-weight three-month old daughter Mitzi in her hat for this photo taken in 1928. Tad Lucas took her daughter to all the rodeos. At six, Mitzi Riley took up riding and performing. National Cowgirl Museum and Hall of Fame.

Many cowgirl costumes were home-made, and others were custom orders from saddleries. This unidentified cowgirl wears an unusual outfit of patchwork hair-on cowhide, c. 1930. National Cowboy Hall of Fame.

performances. Kitty Canutt had a diamond set into her front tooth for both style and insurance against lean times. Outside the arena, cowgirls consistently dressed with flair. When Pearl Mason, World Champion bronc rider in 1918, was not in the saddle, she wore a rattlesnake coat made from the skins of snakes she had either killed herself or had received as gifts from places as distant as California, Nevada, New Mexico, and Old Mexico.

In the early 1920s, cowgirls started to copy men's styles as an alternative to modifying women's fashions. Thus pants came into vogue around the year 1925. McGinnis's idea to wear pants was conceived after she had watched Will Rogers and his family perform at the Ambassador Horse Show in Southern California. Mary Rogers wore long white-flannel pants exactly like those of her brothers. "They looked so neat and easy to work in compared with the tight breeches we wore, I thought, why not?," McGinnis wrote. "Mary was just a little girl, but it should still be alright for slight-built girls like myself to wear them."

"Skirts were such a nuisance," McGinnis said. With her mother, she sat down at her sewing machine and created a pair of customized trousers from a pair of little boys' flannel pants with a new zipper on the side. "I wore them for the first time at the Fort Worth Fat Stock Show that spring, and they were a hit," she says. "Later in Europe, I had my complete new wardrobe fashioned with long pants. When I returned to the states I found that many of the girls had followed my lead. Long pants were definitely in."

McGinnis adored her white satin pants accented with silver cord and worn with a sleeveless bolero trimmed in gold and silver braid. With this ensemble she wore a bright-red blouse and sash and her trademark mammoth white Stetson. "It was my best outfit, and I felt very chic as I dashed into the arena smiling," she said. About wearing pants, McGinnis also remarked: "I like to wear them so then I can kick up my heels as I like."

Another fashion plate in the 1920s was Tad Lucas. She learned to sew after her big spill when she fell from her trick-riding horse and hurt her arm. "Since I couldn't ride," she said, "I decided that I would learn to sew. I had never been much of a seamstress." But Lucas caught on and selected all her fabrics from mills in New York. "Even then," she commented, "whipcord was sixteen dollars per yard, but a suit made of whipcord lasted forever. There was no wear-out to it."

Lucas made velvet suits and attached brilliant trim with her own rhinestone machine. She was also a fan of woolly chaps, made of Angora hair, which caught everybody's fancy. Rodeo cowgirls were proud and their clothes reflected their spirited confidence. "We all had lots of clothes," Lucas said. "We always wore our best clothes, no matter what we were doing. If we had to ride a bull or a bucking horse or anything else, we wore our best clothes, we sure did."

This studio photograph of Mabel Strickland was taken by famous rodeo photographer, Ralph Doubleday. The elegant pose and costume were undoubtedly inspired by Hollywood fashions of the 1930s. National Cowboy Hall of Fame.

A Gene Krieg Creed trophy for "Champion Cowgirl Bronc Rider" in 1930, and a trophy won by Mary Parks in 1937, sit with a number of Vera McGinnis's trophies from California, the Pendleton Round-up, and England. National Cowgirl Museum and Hall of Fame.

(right) Vera McGinnis poses here with trophies she won in Ireland, France, and Belgium in 1925 in Tex Austin's rodeo. She enjoyed her fame. "I earned it and took it gracefully," she said. "No other girl had been in so many other countries or shown western riding and the western style of life. No one's been where I've been. I was there." National Cowgirl Museum and Hall of Fame.

(opposite) Vera McGinnis's rodeo career started in 1913 in Salt Lake City, Utah. In her first relay race her horse crashed into one of the other contestants, a faux pas leaving McGinnis in last place with a headache and one missing tooth. The producers were nevertheless impressed and signed her up for a rodeo tour of Canada. McGinnis went on to become a champion cowgirl, Hollywood star, and fashion trendsetter. Her career ended in 1935 with a fall that punctured her lung and broke her hip, neck, back, and most of her ribs. She was told she would probably die and would definitely never walk again. She defied the odds by walking out of the hospital a few months later. National Cowgirl Museum and Hall of Fame.

Cowgirls, sporting 1930s fashions in the form of bell-bottom pants, pose for a picture. In just ten years, cowgirls changed from unique homemade outfits to this more standard uniform. Cowboy Hall of Fame.

Cowgirls looked their best, even when they were competing in rough-stock events. Lucyle Richards (left) is shown here in a fancy white costume with her friend and champion bronc rider, Alice Greenough, c. 1930s. Prairie Rose Collection.

A cowgirl's buckskin draw-string purse, similar to the one carried by Alice Greenough, c. 1925. Slaughter Collection.

142

This rodeo banner, measuring eight feet in width, probably decorated an announcer's stand during the 1930s. It is unusual that a cowgirl on a bucking horse sporting a six-shooter was used for this type of rodeo decoration. Hengesbaugh Collection.

Images of the cowgirl and cowboy were used in tandem for a wide variety of western and rodeo merchandise. This felt banner decorated with a cowgirl rope-spinner was created for the Texas Centennial in 1936. Holley Collection.

After rodeos excluded cowgirls from rough-stock events, they invited women to return as rodeo queens. These women helped promote the rodeos with their beauty but unfortunately not with their skill. As shown on this 1940s rodeo program, the cowgirl had become much more of a glamour girl than a competitor. Harman Collection.

143

"Learning Western Ways," a hand-tinted
photograph by Jackson Hole photographer
Harrison R. Crandall, c. 1930. Many eastern
dudes arrived in the West in their tweed
riding outfits and were shortly
transformed into cowgirls. This
romanticized photograph features the
Westerner talking to the Easterner in front
of the Grand Teton Mountains in Jackson
Hole, Wyoming. Flood Collection.

DUDES & ROMANCE

CHAPTER 4

When Countess Eleanor Patterson, her daughter Felicia, and their French maid arrived at the Victor, Idaho depot in 1916, they were uncertain whether they would enjoy their stay in the Wild West. The sign on the hotel read LOBY; inside were some noisy cowboys who shot tobacco into brass spittoons, and dinner at the hotel was as appetizing as "boiled bedroom slippers." After a fitful sleep, the trio journeyed ten hours by wagon over Teton Pass to Jackson Hole, Wyoming. Settling into the rustic cabins on the Bar BC dude ranch, they yearned for the warmth and luxuries of their Washington, D.C. home. Their rooms had no running water or electricity. The cabins were so small that their six trunks packed with petticoats and fancy frocks had to remain outside.

Despite the initial shock, the Countess, titled from her previous marriage to Count Gizycki of Poland, and her companions were enthusiastic about life at the Bar BC, Jackson Hole's second dude ranch. Like many other well-to-do Easterners who traveled to the Rocky Mountains in search of a western adventure, these ladies were bewitched by a curiously civilized country where cowboys courted debutantes, shoot-outs occurred, and life was lived to the fullest (often on the back of a mustang). In those years between 1880 and 1930, a trip West was as exotic as an African safari. "Things were rugged here," one old-timer recalls of the early days in Jackson Hole. "The law was such that people didn't bother with it. Everyone did as they pleased."

Women were particularly intrigued with dude ranching. Perhaps seeing Annie Oakley or some rodeo cowgirls nurtured their self-images as cowgirls. Alternatively, a ranch romance novel, a "B" Western, Owen Wister's *Virginian*, or Emerson Hough's *North of 36*, the story of a ranch woman who drives her herd north, could have inspired a trip west. In particular, equestrians looked forward to galloping horses across open meadows and winding through evergreen

This illustration for the famous Valley Ranch, one of the most prestigious dude ranches in Cody, Wyoming at the turn of the century, portrays a well-dressed dude girl from the early 1920s. Lebel Collection.

Eastern dudes arrived at the train depot and were often transported in fancy coaches to the more elegant dude ranches during the first decades of the 1900s. These Easterners are on their way to Eatons' Ranch in Wolf, Wyoming in 1918. Shields Collection.

Dude ranching became a well-organized industry by the early 1920s. Often the railroad companies helped to promote a family vacation with attractive brochures listing ranches and activities.

This clever postcard of the early 1940s features a stylized cowgirl inappropriately dressed for ranch life. Painter Collection.

forests. Whatever the stimulus, these women anticipated adventure. Nannie Alderson, who married a cowboy, soon discovered that Westerners were more interested in one's character than one's pedigree. "Half the charm of the country for me was its broad-mindedness. I loved it from the first," Alderson wrote in her book *A Bride Goes West*. "I hadn't needed to come to Montana to find out that a new country offered greater personal liberty than an old and settled one."

In the early days a dude was usually an "Easterner," often from a prominent family. Other variations on the word included dudine, describing a lady, and dudette, referring to a child (usually a girl). Dude ranchers insisted that the word "dude" was not pejorative; it was used originally to describe a guest who was not from the West and who paid to stay on a western ranch or to engage the services of a guide.

The promise of "roughing it" in the wild, sleeping in the mountains under a canopy of stars, and living like a cowboy intrigued the dudes. Ranches were difficult to reach, and cabins were rustic. The privy was usually a short jaunt across the sage. While some ranches had both cattle and guests, others were strictly set up for entertainment—riding, roping, and campfire socializing. On the early dude ranch, the host, several wranglers, a cabin girl or maid, and that all-important person the cook, catered to the needs of ten to thirty paying guests. The dudes, who often stayed a month or an entire summer, were enfolded in a welcoming atmosphere. The dude rancher was king along this frontier and, according to the Bar BC brochure and many other ranch advertisements, guests also could be ejected if they proved not to the host's liking.

Many women traveled to ranches on their own or with a girlfriend. After arriving *via* the Union Pacific Railroad, and later in their own Model Ts, young women from the East discarded their city dresses and changed into cowgirl clothing. Most likely they purchased boots, broad-brimmed hats, split skirts, beaded Indian vests, and later Levis at the ranch store or in a nearby town. Like the rodeo cowgirls, they also tied a silk scarf around their necks. Dudes who returned to a ranch summer after summer sometimes sported the brand of their ranch on their boots or on a pair of spurs. Because western clothing was useless at home, they often left their gear in a trunk at the ranch to be used when they returned.

Inspired by Wild West shows or the movies, dudines relished the flamboyance and originality of the Western style and hoped to blend in with the Westerners—an almost impossible task. "The sign of acclimation of a dude was

Wealthy Easterners arrived at the
Valley Ranch in Cody, Wyoming for
a summer of riding, fishing in blue-
ribbon trout streams, and sleeping in
rustic cabins. These affluent dudes
could afford the best saddles, spurs,
and other western finery available.
Buffalo Bill Historical Center.

(below and right) Dudes fancied
western jewelry such as silver
and gold bandana slides. They
also accented their outfits with
gold jewelry purchased from
Edward Bohlin and other makers.
The necklace features an elk tooth.
High Noon Collection.

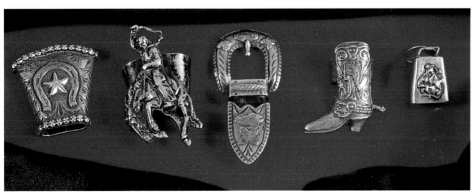

Fashion was an important part of the dudine's ranch experience. Many of these women purchased riding outfits from local saddleries and sometimes from the Indians. Some of the outfits were made by New York companies such as Abercrombie and Fitch or Brooks Brothers. Buffalo Bill Historical Center.

For rodeos and other special dude-ranch events, many of the guests commissioned local companies to make outfits such as this fringed skirt with a horse head outlined in brass harness spots, c. 1920. King Collection.

frequently the degree to which he adapted himself to Western costume and looked at home in it," Nathaniel Burt wrote in his book *Jackson Hole Journal*, "but even the most seasoned dude tended to look a bit different somehow—a bit less taut, a little less swagger." Nevertheless, dudes acquired their own distinct but charming style. As Wyoming dude rancher Emily Oliver once said proudly, "You're a dude 'till you die."

Dudes spent their days riding horses in the mountains, shared home-cooked meals and conversation, and slept in rough-hewn but cozy cabins or out-of-doors. A wrangler at the corral determined their riding ability and selected a compatible horse for each guest. Rides were offered daily, often with the exception of Sunday, which was a day of rest for the dude ponies. Other activities included fishing, watching wildlife, visiting national parks, sometimes working cattle, and—the ultimate dude experience—a pack trip into the wilderness. "What fun we had," wrote Mary Shawver about her first pack trip at the turn of the century. "Days of thrills and evenings about the great campfire. All slept as never before breathing air laden with the scent of pine and the sagebrush. Occasionally during the night a Roman candle or rocket would flare as it was sent up to frighten the bears away from the cook wagon."

Men as well as women relished the beauty and simplicity of this life, far from the stresses of the world they had left behind, if only for a short while. Victorian travelers also enjoyed the unconventional informality of ranch life, which encouraged men, women, and their families to mingle socially. "Anticipation often surpasses realization but that is not true of this great region," wrote Shawver, who moved West and became a partner at the Holm Lodge in Cody, Wyoming for thirty-five years. "It is not possible to anticipate the fullness of it. Only experience can give the joys and thrills of the magnificent panorama of nature at its best."

The West overwhelmed those accustomed to more civilized environments. Isabella L. Bird, a British lady who traveled on horseback in 1873 throughout Colorado and visited some of the ranches in that country, relished the West's intoxicating beauty and profound silence. In her book, *A Lady's Life in the Rocky Mountains*, Bird wrote: "The scenery up here is glorious, combining sublimity with beauty, and in the elastic air fatigue has dropped off from me. This is no region for tourists and women, only for a few elk and bear hunters at times, and its unprofaned freshness gives me new life."

This buckskin riding outfit includes a fringed riding skirt and matching bolero vest. The outfit belonged to journalist and author Caroline Lockhart, a friend of Buffalo Bill's and a long-time Cody, Wyoming resident. After Lockhart visited Cody, Wyoming in 1904 at the age of twenty-three, she moved there to continue a successful writing career begun in Boston, New York, and Philadelphia. In 1921 she published her novel The Dude Wrangler, which promoted the beneficial aspects of dude ranching. Autry Museum of Western Heritage.

A staged photo of Annice Belden taken by her husband and well-known photographer, Charles Belden, of the Pitchfork Ranch in Cody, Wyoming illustrates a dudine's dream: fly fishing with her pony in the Greybull River on the Belden ranch. Belden Museum.

The Valley Ranch in Cody, Wyoming promoted summer camping trips on horseback for parties composed entirely of young girls. The clear mountain air was a healthy alternative to the industrial city environment in which many of these wealthy girls lived. Buffalo Bill Historical Center.

(opposite top) This romantic illustration depicts a cowgirl and her alert pony in an isolated valley. Illustrations such as this one beckoned Eastern girls to experience the West. Walden Collection.

(opposite bottom) A photo by Harrison R. Crandall, c. 1930, shows a confident young dudine ready to head into the wilderness on a fine horse. Buffalo Bill Historical Center.

Romance in these idyllic surroundings was unavoidable. Sparks between the sophisticated lady and the cowboy flew so frequently on a dude ranch that courting might have been part of the wrangler's job description. As Nathaniel Burt wrote in *Jackson Hole Journal*, "It was the remoteness that did it. There was nobody around to mediate between the dudes and the roughnecks, countesses and cowboys, shut up together in their cantankerous Shangri-La."

Mary Shawver reports that one of her guests believed young girls "fell in love with their horses and as they could not marry a horse they married the man who smelled like a horse." When questioned about dude-cowboy love affairs, one dude rancher rolled his eyes and said: "There was a lot of that."

"You fell in love with someone every year," said Dorothy King, an Eatons' Ranch dude for years who finally married her cowboy, Don King, owner of the renowned Sheridan saddlery. Patterson—debutante, Countess, editor of the *Washington Herald*—found her Virginian when she fell in love with

Cal Carrington, the wrangler at the Bar BC. Thoroughly taken with the West—its rugged landscape and honest people, Patterson purchased her own Jackson Hole ranch and hired Carrington as her manager. They spent a romantic hunting trip together at Soda Fork where, confined to their tent on snowy days, Patterson read aloud from *War and Peace*. After many days of riding together in Jackson Hole, she transported Carrington to her mansion in Washington, D.C., where visitors admired him like a fine daVinci and the butler scurried behind him with a spittoon. Their relationship was "one of the most flamboyant dude-cowboy affairs," wrote Nathaniel Burt.

Eastern women fell for the Western man because he was refreshingly different from men they had previously known. He was both clever and comfortable in his native surroundings, had common sense, a rugged demeanor, and a quiet, understated sense of humor. Even the cowgirls understood the attraction to the cowboy. "I like Eastern men," said Miss Wyoming Helene Bonham, "but they are altogether different from the ones of the West. They are more clever and they talk more—but when a Western man tells you something you know he has his brand on it, and he means it. When I choose, it will be from the West."

A well-worn pair of children's cowboy boots, featuring red hearts and clubs, c. 1930. Benson Collection.

Perhaps not surprisingly, many of these relationships endured; other love affairs ended sadly. A chore boy from a Montana ranch fell in love with one of the fancy guests from Boston. Riding behind him in beautiful, open country, she experienced a similar infatuation. The following autumn in Boston marked a return to the cotillion crowd and a rapidly fading memory of that summer in the West, until the day that Roy appeared at her doorstep.

"What are you doing here?" she asked, obviously surprised.

Despite admonishment from the boss, Roy had quit his ranch job and had spent all his earnings on a ticket to the East coast. Beaming, he said, "You told me you'd love me forever." There was a long silence, then "Oh Roy, you know I was just kidding," before she shut the door. The penniless Roy hitchhiked back

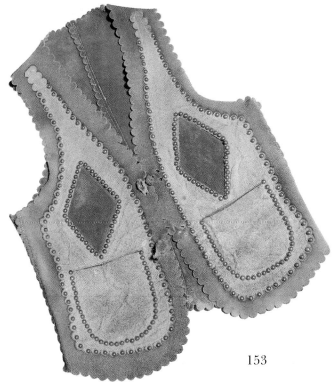

Children enjoyed playing cowboy on a dude ranch. Shown here are red cowhide chaps featuring the Indian symbol for good luck outlined with nickel harness spots, and a child's pair of hair-on cowhide batwing chaps made by Keyston Bros., c. 1935. Toy holsters, a hat and boots, and a saddle completed a child's dude-ranch outfit. Walden/Benson Collections.

An unmarked spotted and split cowhide child's vest, c. 1935. Hengesbaugh Collection.

Buckskin riding gauntlets with Indian beaded decoration were a popular dudine accessory. This Plateau Indian pair has a cowgirl depicted on a bucking horse, c. 1915. Schmitt/Cayuse Collection.

Hats were always an important part of a cowgirl's outfit. This Stetson has a Carlsbad crease and beaded hatband. The swastika frequently decorated cowboy gear prior to World War II. Flood Collection.

(opposite) Dude-girl outfits were inspired by cowgirls who rode in rodeo or in Wild West shows. This woman, probably a western performer, sports a style imitated by dudines, i.e., beaded gauntlets, a silk scarf, leather skirt, silk shirt, and hat. Schmitt/Cayuse Collection.

155

Many cowgirls wore buckskin riding gloves decorated with fancy embroidery. The lone star was an indication that the wearer originated from Texas, c. 1910-1920. Lebel Collection.

Nothing more set a cowgirl apart from mere mortals than her hat. They came in a wide variety of shapes and colors. The style of crown often disclosed the geographic origin of the wearer. From 1910 throughout the 1930s, the larger the brim and the taller the crown, the more desirable was the hat. Luevand Collection.

These fashionable dudines are wearing a combination of elegant East coast riding outfits mixed with beaded Indian vests, gloves, and jewelry. While most dude ranchers knew that these women did not look exactly like cowgirls, they encouraged western dress because, as well-known dude rancher Struthers Burt said, "it is good for their souls." Buffalo Bill Historical Center.

Dudines would purchase fancy beaded vests from local Indians who lived near the dude ranches. The types of patterns signified the tribal origin of the piece. This unusual Indian-beaded pictorial vest, c. 1920, features two horse heads. (Schmitt/Cayuse Collection). The other vest, beaded in a rose pattern, was typical of styles sold at trading posts or at dude ranch stores. Williams Collection.

A Harrison R. Crandall photograph of a dude string returning to the Triangle X Ranch, c. 1930. Horseback riding on mountain trails was one of the most popular activities on any dude ranch. Dude ranchers purchased horses that gave the inexperienced rider a sense of security but nonetheless appeared challenging. Dude string horses usually were called Pokey, Rose, or Spot, but when the dudes arrived at the beginning of the season, wranglers would rechristen the ponies with more menacing epithets such as Lightening, Thunder, or Dynamite. Teton County Historical Society.

Many dudines became excellent riders by the end of the summer and were consequently given more spirited, athletic horses. Flood Collection.

Dudes gather in the living room of the 4-K Ranch in Dean, Montana, c. 1950. The furnishings had remained untouched since the beginning of this ranch in 1930. The room features a Thomas Molesworth couch and pole furniture made by E. Rathe of Montana. Fighting Bear Antiques Collection.

Dude-ranch owners decorated their cabin floors with Navajo rugs and saddle blankets. This Navajo pictorial saddle blanket, c. 1910, features an elaborate horse and rolling log design. Schmitt/Cayuse Collection.

Horn accessories were popular decorative items at ranches. Intrigued with this rustic cowboy style, many dudes purchased Western furniture for their houses "back East." Hunn Collection.

Thomas Molesworth of Cody, Wyoming built rustic furniture from 1930-1950. He was well-known for his pieces built with burled wood and upholstered in leather or with Chimayo wool cushions. Molesworth, whose name has become as well known as the American furniture designer Gustav Stickley, furnished many Wyoming and Montana ranches, and his work continues to be popular. High Noon Collection.

159

(opposite top) **This fancy leather split riding skirt, with its patch pockets, conchas, and abundant fringe, would have been a premium riding skirt in the 1920s. High Noon Collection.**

(opposite bottom) **Elegant young dudines are decked out in English riding breeches, leather-fringed riding skirts, and beaded vests. Dudes enjoyed dressing up at dude ranches and, like the old-time cowgirl, they embraced conspicuous attire. Buffalo Bill Historical Center.**

Wealthy dudes could afford fine boots and would often order a custom-made pair decorated with fancy leather inlays, c. 1920. Schmitt/Cayuse Collection.

This dudine's hat is decorated with a whipped leather edge and a Blackfeet Indian hatband. Schmitt/Cayuse Collection.

A young dudine would have been quite stylish in this fancy ranch outfit. It consisted of riding pants, beaded vest, custom boots, and a fancy Stetson, c. 1930. Schmitt/Cayuse Collection.

Fancy cowgirl boots with colorful floral overlays and hand-painted accents, c. 1940. Sage Collection.

A premium pair of boots decorated with arrows and Indians wearing war bonnets. High Noon Collection.

(right) The golden age of the cowboy boot was 1920-1950. In these few decades cowboy boots became a leather canvas for the boot maker's art. Popular embellishments included butterflies, flowers, and eagles. Both men and women wore these flamboyant designs. Luevand Collection.

Until the 1930s boots were typically worn outside the pants, and the uppers were heavily decorated. These cowgirl boots, made by Nocona Boot Co. (Nocona, Texas), c. 1940, are decorated with the popular butterfly design. Flashy boots were very popular with dudes. Sage Collection.

Dudine Liz Ludlow of Springfield, Ohio, accompanied by her sister Kathryn, visited Eatons' Ranch from 1919-1928. Daughter of a wealthy industrialist, Ludlow could afford the best. She commissioned Rex Schnitger, a well-known bit and spur maker living in Gillette, Wyoming, to make these classic Wyoming-style, silver-mounted spurs, c. 1920. Ludlow's name and Eaton Ranch are written on the spur straps. Butters Collection.

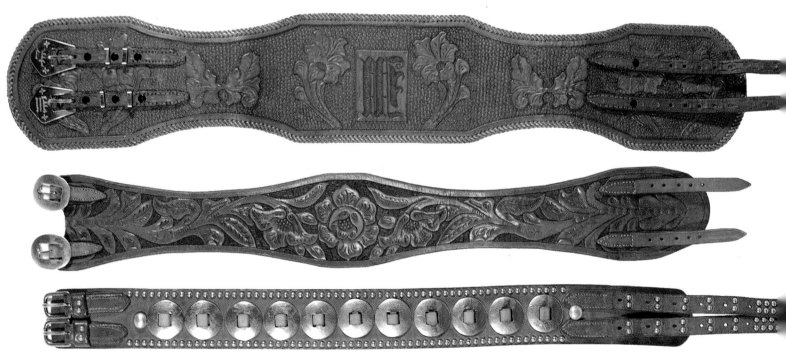

(above) **Dudines purchased fancy embroidered western shirts for parties that were held weekly at the dude ranches. Old and new embroidered shirts continue to be popular. High Noon Collection.**

Elegant western fashion had been part of a dude cowgirl's western experience from the first days of dude ranching, as illustrated in this hand-colored Harrison R. Crandall photograph. Schmitt/Cayuse Collection.

(opposite top) **Dude girls loved flashy western belts. They were often made of engraved leather, beadwork, or hitched horsehair. Buckles were often sterling silver, c. 1920-1940. High Noon Collection.**

(opposite bottom) **These wide cowgirl belts with detailed engraving and conchas were adapted from bronc buster belts and would have been worn for special occasions, such as local rodeos or parties, c. 1920. Schmitt/Cayuse Collection.**

Women visiting dude ranches were always fascinated by cowboys. Perhaps their allure lay in their woolly chaps, but most likely it was their independent, self-assured nature that intrigued these eastern socialites. Buffalo Bill Historical Center.

Dudines dreamed of riding off across the prairie alongside their cowboy sweethearts, as illustrated in this calendar art, c. 1930. DeBeer Collection.

to Montana, whereupon he resumed duties at the dude ranch. For many of the dudines, playing cowgirl was strictly a summer-time role.

Many ranchers maintain that dude ranching started as a party among friends. When entertaining friends became expensive, families charged their frequent guests. Cattle ranchers often took in guests to supplement their income, and other travelers engaged native guides to take them on pack trips. Throughout Montana, Wyoming, and Colorado, a few entrepreneurs set up hunting camps to entice tourists to the West. Soon these pack trip outfits developed into dude operations, and hunting camps expanded to accommodate women and children.

Many historians cite the year 1882 as the beginning of dude ranching, when Bert Rumsey of Buffalo, New York, wanted to pay Howard, Alden, and Willis Eaton to stay at their Custer Trail cattle ranch in Medora, North Dakota. "I'm having a good time. I need the outdoor life. I don't want to go home. I've got plenty of money and I'd consider it a favor if you'd let me stay awhile and pay something each week for my board and the use of a horse,"

Hearts have always been a popular decoration with cowgirls. Many a cowboy branded a calf with a heart as a symbol of his love for his cowgirl sweetheart. Benson Collection.

167

Quirts were a western style of riding whip that was frequently made of hitched horsehair. This one was made by the daughter-in-law of Cochise, the great Apache chief of the late 1800s. Cowgirls were often seen with a quirt looped over their wrist. Benson Collection.

Many an East coast socialite dreamed of living in the mountains and marrying a cowboy. A surprising number of women made their dream come true. DeBeer Collection.

Rumsey told Howard Eaton. Subsequently Rumsey signed the Eatons' guest register and paid ten dollars a week for a ranch experience. Dude ranching was most popular in Wyoming, Montana, and Colorado, but dude ranches exist in California, Arizona, New Mexico, Washington, Oregon, Utah, and Texas.

From the beginning, the ranches that combined "Eastern" thinking with "Western" common sense and expertise succeeded. While the Easterner knew the clientele, it was the Westerner who provided a safe experience for the greenhorn. The early dude ranches, such as Eatons' Ranch in Sheridan, the Valley in Cody, and the Bar BC, were all run by highly educated Eastern folks with an understanding of western living.

"It is good for both the Westerner and Easterner to know each other, and once the initial embarrassment is over and the provincialism on both sides dissipated, the Easterner and Westerner as a rule like each other. And, where the Easterner is concerned, much is lost in a visit to a ranch if he fails to learn something about the people who live on the ranches," wrote Bar BC dude rancher Struthers Burt in *Diary of a Dude Wrangler*. For dudes, balancing a barbecue and beans over crossed legs was somehow a more real experience than tipping tea cups at the Waldorf-Astoria.

Of course, there were exceptions to the East-West formula. Two Montana rodeo cowgirls, Margo and Violet Brander, started a dude ranch called the Circle Star in Avon, Montana in the 1930s. They understood the importance of sharing their country with dudes as well as the value of a relationship between horse and man. "Of course," Violet Brander said, "an automobile is all right if you're in a hurry to get some place—but most of the really nice places are up in the mountains where no car can go—and who in the heck ever loved an automobile?"

"We'd give em' what they need—plenty of fresh mountain air, plenty of the outside of a horse—the old saying goes that the outside of a horse is good for the insides of a man and I've found that's true of women too-and plenty of good, well cooked food," Margo Brander added.

A dude ranch was always much more than a summer hotel. "Unaware as dudes may be of this fact, there is a social and moral and actual responsibility unlike any responsibility attached to the job of being a hotel keeper," wrote Struthers Burt. A dude rancher is responsible for everyone's happiness. Burt knew the ingredients: "If you wish to sum up the dude business in one sentence, it consists in giving people home-made bedsteads but forty-pound mattresses."

A dude ranch vacation continues to be a popular destination for city folk. On these oases where the myth and the reality of the West are integrated, the wranglers might adopt a fancier dress code than that of a working hand,

Many commercial products featured cowgirls with their cowboy sweethearts, as is illustrated on this cigar tin, c. 1905. Benson Collection.

A tourist postcard of a western couple, c. 1905-1910.

Well-known cowboy and cowgirl couple Chet and Juanita Howell hold hands in the arena at a fair and rodeo in Centralia, Washington, for their wedding photograph, August 9, 1936. Their wedding was the feature attraction of the night show. Monty Montana and his wife Louise were the best man and matron of honor, respectively. National Cowgirl Museum and Hall of Fame.

Illustrated cards were premiums in Hassen cigarettes, c. 1910. This card features cowboy courtship. Bachman Collection.

The cowboy and cowgirl were romanticized as the perfect American couple at the turn of the century. The postcard reads: "All nature seems to speak to me of you."

A cowboy kisses his sweetheart, c. 1900. Schmitt/Cayuse Collection.

A popular image was the cowgirl gazing into the campfire with her cowboy sweetheart, as depicted in this turn-of-the-century print. Holly Collection.

Because of the scarcity of women in the rural areas of the West, cowboys always had great respect for their cowgirl sweethearts. This sentiment is obvious in this turn-of-the-century postcard. Painter Collection.

Copyright 1907 by W. G. M.   Cowboy Series—"Broken In."

but they nevertheless provide the expertise expected by the dudes. The food is wholesome, and the hosts spoil their guests with the legendary western hospitality. Dudes dress like Westerners, ride the range, and appreciate the unparalleled beauty of the mountains and sunsets. Despite the best of intentions on the part of the management, romance continues over the fence between the dudines and the wranglers. For many non-westerners, the dude ranch is a place where a broader love affair with the West finds its beginning. And, as Shawver recognized, dudes learn about themselves.

"After the life in such inspiring surroundings all go home with new views on old ways of life." Mary Shawver wrote. "They have a new personality that carries them on, able to get more out of life because they are putting more of their better selves into it."

Valentine Greetings

V-63

SAY WHEN READY AND I'LL SHOOT.

I don't mind bein' roped in by the right gal.

GEE! DIS IS HEAVEN—
TO BE SIMPLY ALONE
ALL ALONE
ALONE

Ropin' cattle's one thing gals is another

Your heart is mine — my Valentine

Cowboy and cowgirl love has long been portrayed on Valentine's cards and postcards. The illustrations typically depict cowboys roping in their love or getting a drop on their sweetheart with their six-shooter, c. 1900-1910. Painter Collection.

At last I've roped you in
And have you safely tied.
Now for a life that's happy:
Come, be a Cow Boy's Bride.

B 2636

PHOTO ONLY COPYRIGHT 1908
BY THE ROTOGRAPH CO.

B 2637

I'm happy to be lassoed
By so sweet a girl as you,
Let's join our lives together
And live near the mountains blue.

PHOTO ONLY COPYRIGHT 1908
BY THE ROTOGRAPH CO.

I dont care if the hull outfit
stampedes I'll stay by you

I'd like ter round up a Valentine and brand her with my Heart.

Whom do you love, pard ?

CARL LAEMMLE, OFFERS

MARIE WALCAMP

IN

TEMPEST CODY RIDES WILD

ONE OF THE FAMOUS

"SPUR AND SADDLE" STORIES

DIRECTED BY JACQUES JACCARD

HOLLYWOOD

CHAPTER 5

Since the famous "first" western movie, *The Great Train Robbery*, starring Broncho Billy Anderson, made its debut in 1903, cowboy heroes have continued their easily-won dominance. In theaters across the country, boys cheered when a man "packing iron" and wearing a Stetson galloped across the silver screen to capture the bad guy, and subsequently, the (good) girl. After the film, boys (and a few tomboys) returned to their backyards, donned hats, and played favorite heroes such as William S. Hart, Tom Mix, Hoot Gibson, Buck Jones, and later, John Wayne, Gene Autry, Hopalong Cassidy, and Roy Rogers. Little has been written about the cowgirl stars and their fans. Young women looked up to independent cowgirl characters played by Barbara Stanwyck and Dale Evans in the 1940s and 1950s. Who were the stars before these women? Surprisingly, Hollywood was well-populated with leading cowgirl stars and *real* cowgirls.

During the silent era (1895-1930), a number of actresses played cowgirls who, like the early ranch women and rodeo competitors, had pluck and charm. Actresses such as Ruth Roland, Helen Gibson, Texas Guinan, Marin Sais, Ann Little, Marie Walcamp, and Evelyn Selbie received top billing above the cowboy and his horse in hundreds of films. Many of these women performed their own stunts—they rode horses at breakneck speed, fired guns, and captured the outlaws. Marguerite Clayton, the first "Broncho Billy Girl", starred in one-reelers (1909-1915) with Broncho Billy Anderson. Ann Little, a California ranch girl nicknamed "the Darling of the Plains," also worked with Anderson, but Evelyn Selbie, who performed with him from 1912 to 1915, is remembered as his leading lady. Cowgirls thrived on the action and the excitement generated in Hollywood. Born in Denison, Ohio in 1884, Marie Walcamp was best known for her *Tempest Cody* series in 1919, which featured bronco-busting, shoot-outs, romance, and many cross-country pursuits at a full gallop. "There was something magnetic in the click-click of

This sexy pose of a Hollywood cowgirl starlet was popular during the 1940s. High Noon Collection.

(opposite) Marie Walcamp, the reigning serial queen in 1919, made dozens of Westerns, films that could be shot in two days and featured plenty of action. Walcamp thrived on her work despite the predictability of the scripts. "Of course, it's always the same old thing, I get chased, abused, nearly killed, rescued in the nick of time, loved, hated—and finally there's the happy forever after!" she was quoted in Motion Picture Classics, 1920. Pokrifcsak Collection.

the camera—it made me want to get out in front of it and do stunts," said Walcamp in the 1919 issue of *Motion Picture Magazine.* "I wanted to see myself in action—to see myself as others saw me."

Texas Guinan (Mary Louise Cecelia Guinan), another cowgirl star of the early two-reelers, grew up on a ranch near Waco, Texas. She had studied art and music in Chicago but had returned to the Rocky Mountains to compete in rodeo. In 1911, she won the World's Championship Bronco Riding title at the Cheyenne round-up. After working for the Miller Brothers' 101 Ranch, she landed the lead role in *The Gun Woman* (1918). Advertisements for the film read: "Never Jilt a Woman Who Can Shoot." She continued in film, often billed as "The Female William Hart" or the "two-gun tigress," and believed herself to be the equal of any "tobacco-chewin' cowpoke." In 1921, Guinan organized her own Texas Guinan Productions and produced and starred in a number of western shorts. "I got twelve real cowboys, a scenario writer [Mildred Sledge], a cameraman, a carload of cartridges, my horse 'Waco' from Texas, and went to work. We made a picture a week," she said. "We never changed plots, only horses." After doing her own stunts in 300 movies, Guinan moved to New York City in 1924, where she donned feminine attire, ran speakeasies, and was arrested forty-nine times.

Other cowgirl stars became heroines to their audiences. In *The Secret of Lost Valley* (1917), Marin Sais played the part of a young woman belonging to an old Spanish ranching family. She not only pursued a villain on horseback, but lassoed him and delivered him to the authorities. Ruth Roland, who became popular through appearances in hundreds of serials, seduced audiences with her courage, athletic ability, and her horse Joker. Roland dressed in a giant felt hat, a checked shirt, and batwing

Like prominent Western stars Tom Mix and Buck Jones, Mabel Normand (1898-1930) was said to have been discovered at the 101 Ranch in Oklahoma. She went on to become a great comedienne on the silent screen. Normand started her film career at sixteen in 1910 with Vitagraph and Biograph studios. She became a star with Mack Sennett, and later with Goldwyn Mayer Studios. This is an unusual photograph because Normand did very few Westerns. Schmitt/Cayuse Collection.

Marie Walcamp, born in Denison, Ohio on July 17, 1894, was a popular silent movie cowgirl from the mid-teens through the mid-1920s. Walcamp was best known for her "Tempest Cody" series in which she played a tough, adventure-seeking cowgirl. Rainey Collection.

(opposite) A capable cowgirl roping a steer is the main subject for this movie poster used in 1912 to promote a film about the life of Buffalo Bill. Buffalo Bill Historical Center.

(right and bottom) **Olive Fuller Golden Carey, a rodeo performer and early silent movie cowgirl, is shown here both with and without makeup. At the age of sixteen or seventeen she appeared in D.W. Griffith's The Sorrowful Shore (1913) with Harry Carey, whom she married three years later. She continued to appear in Westerns, including several with her husband, who was a mentor for film star John Wayne. After her husband died in 1947, Carey starred in The Searchers (1956), Two Rode Together (1961), and The Alamo (1960). Rainey Collection.**

Silent screen actress Josie Sedgwick from Galveston, Texas appeared in a number of two-reel Westerns produced by Universal Studios. Although she was not as famous as her sister, actress Eileen Sedgwick, she did appear on vending cards distributed by the Exhibitors Supply Company along with popular stars Ruth Roland and Pearl White. She retired from movies in 1932. Rainey Collection.

178

Ruth Roland of San Francisco starred in eleven serials, of which nine were Westerns, during the 'teens and twenties. These films featured Roland performing death-defying horseback escapes on her famous horse, Joker. During this time Roland made $2,000 per week. A good actress as well as a shrewd business-woman, Roland amassed a seven-million-dollar fortune before the crash of 1929.

An African-American cowgirl was featured on this poster for The Crimson Skull with an "all colored" cast. Filmed in Jacksonville, Florida in 1923, the movie also featured Bill Pickett, the famous 101 Ranch bulldogger. Pokrifcsak Collection.

THE NORMAN FILM MFG CO.
PRESENTS

'THE CRIMSON SKULL'
BAFFLING WESTERN MYSTERY PHOTOPLAY
CO-STARRING
ANITA BUSH   AND THE VERSATILE
LITTLE MOTHER of COLORED DRAMA   LAWRENCE CHENAULT
Supported by BILL PICKETT, World's Champion Wild West Performer
The One Legged Marvel STEVE REYNOLDS and 30 Colored Cowboys

ALL COLORED CAST   6 SMASHING REELS
PRODUCED BY
NORMAN FILM MFG CO.
JACKSONVILLE, FLA.

Eileen Sedgwick starred in The Girl in the Saddle, made in 1921 by Universal. Sometimes Sedgwick worked on the screen with her sister Josie. Both of these Texas women were cowgirls first and actresses second. Their movies concentrated on action and de-emphasized plot. Rainey Collection.

UNIVERSAL WESTERN

EILEEN SEDGWICK
IN
"The GIRL IN THE SADDLE"

DIRECTED BY
EDDIE KULL

179

Nell Jones was a trick-rider and roper with the 101 Ranch Wild West Show before she went to Hollywood. She is shown here on one of her horses at the couple's Hollywood ranch. Autry Museum of Western Heritage.

Nell Jones's cowhide riding skirt and matching vest, c. 1925. High Noon Collection.

chaps bearing her initials, RRR. Helen Gibson (Rose August Wenger) from the world of rodeo and Wild West shows, thrilled moviegoers with her railroad adventures in *The Hazards of Helen* (1915-1916). These serials, full of action and suspense, featured Gibson leaping from moving trains, capturing malefactors, and shooting guns. In *The Black Horse Bandit* (1919) Gibson captures the murderer of her father, a local sheriff. The acclaimed Lucille Mulhall is said to have earned a million dollars performing in silent films.

Myrtle Stedman, who starred in Westerns beginning in 1911 with William Duncan and Tom Mix, was highly respected by the cowboys on the set for her competence and charm. They called her "a gal to ride the range with." Edyth Sterling, who rode a bucking bronc in one film, and Betty Harte, who jumped onto a skittish horse in another, also played strong cowgirl leads. In fact, in

William Fox presents *Tom Mix* AND TONY THE WONDER HORSE

IN

"RIDERS OF THE PURPLE SAGE"

BASED ON ZANE GREY'S GREATEST NOVEL

WITH

- MABEL BALLIN - WILFRED LUCAS - BEATRICE BURNHAM -
- MARIAN NIXON - WARNER OLAND - HAROLD GOODWIN -

A LYNN REYNOLDS PRODUCTION

Ruth Mix was the daughter of Hollywood cowboy star Tom Mix. She is shown here spinning a wedding ring with a thirty-foot rope. She performed in rodeo and appeared in several films during the mid-1930s. National Cowboy Hall of Fame.

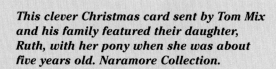

"FOLLOWING IN THE FOOTSTEPS OF HER DAD"

This clever Christmas card sent by Tom Mix and his family featured their daughter, Ruth, with her pony when she was about five years old. Naramore Collection.

A movie still features Victoria Forde in a Western with her husband Tom Mix (middle) and Sid Jourdon (right). Husband-and-wife acting teams were popular in early low-budget Westerns. Producers could often hire a couple at a discount. The wives of cowboy actors were typically ex-rodeo performers and skilled riders. Rainey Collection.

This 1925 poster for William Fox's Riders of the Purple Sage , starring Tom Mix and Beatrice Burnham, features a whip-cracking, masked, hard-riding cowgirl. Pokrifcsak Collection.

(right) A lobby card features Jackie Saunders in Fox's film Drag Harlan, 1920. Saunders starred with William Farnum. Gish Collection.

(bottom right) Ruth Roland impressed a global audience with her performances in Western serials from 1910-1935. She was one of Dale Evans's favorites and an inspiration for other young girls of the times. Roland died of cancer on September 22, 1937.

(below) Texas Guinan, who earned the title "The Female William Hart," was tough on and off the screen. She made a series of Westerns during the mid-teens. Guinan took her profits and operated a speakeasy in New York, where she later boasted of forty-nine arrests.

RUTH ROLAND
IN
"HANDS UP"
A PATHÉ SERIAL
EPISODE N° 1
"THE BRIDE OF THE SUN"
PRODUCED BY ASTRA

184

many Westerns Harte was cast as a boy, although she also performed as a woman with Tom Mix. Betty Miles, an expert horsewoman, appeared quite comfortable galloping through the sagebrush, as did trick-rider and stunt woman Evelyn Finely, called "the reckless female equivalent of Yak Canutt."

In the 1920s, Westerns started to assume the formula that characterizes them today: a cowboy hero, abundant action and gunsmoke, and a defenseless woman requiring rescue. There were, however, a few exceptions to this predictable plot. Ruth Roland, firmly established as the Queen of the Western Serials, continued to receive top billing for playing the strong-willed, self-sufficient woman on the range. At the height of her career in the early 1920s, she was making $2000 *per* week. The popularity of her films induced her to establish her own production company, which distributed her films internationally. Other women recognized for their early cowgirl roles include Eileen and Josie Sedgwick, Marilyn Mills, and Neva Gerber. The Sedgwicks were renowned for their horsemanship. Mills was another competent rider who achieved popularity with her horses Beverly and Star, despite criticism that her riding outstripped her acting. Young audiences loved these heroines. In the 1920s, the Exhibitor Supply Company marketed popular vending card portraits of the famous cowgirls.

Rodeo cowgirls Vera McGinnis, Bertha Blancett, Mabel Strickland, and Ruth Mix, Tom Mix's daughter, found employment off-season in Hollywood. Actresses relished the work, despite harsh conditions and low pay. They traveled on dirt roads in buckboard wagons to distant destinations; they spent countless hours fighting hot weather, dust, and wind, and mingling with ribald cowboys on the sets. Some women made as many as one film *per* week. In the early 1920s, McGinnis earned $8 *per* stunt, in which she doubled for Mary Pickford, Dorothy Phillips, and Norma Talmadge. Later she starred in her own series of twenty-four two-reelers that included the cliff-hangers *The Girl from Flamingo* and *Women's Ways*.

Pioneer cowgirl actress Marguerite Clayton of Salt Lake City, Utah, was popular in the early silent movie era. She made innumerable Westerns with Broncho Billy from 1909-1915. She is shown here with cowboy star Art Acord in the Western film Skyhigh Corral, 1926. Clayton retired in 1928. Rainey Collection.

These custom boots with heart inlays were made for Hollywood star Marion Davies, mistress to publishing tycoon William Randolph Hearst. Davies dressed western and wore these boots at Hearst's ranch in California. Gish Collection.

(right) *In the late 1920s and 1930s, Westerns featured cowboy heros such as Ken Maynard and Jack Hoxie performing macho stunts that invariably included the rescuing of a woman. One of the rules of these early Westerns was that the cowboy could kiss his horse but not the girl. Children who supported these pictures disliked sentimentality. Pokrifcsak Collection.*

Ruth Hall, born in Jacksonville, Florida in 1912, and Ken Maynard starred in Between Fighting Men *in 1932. Hall made only five Westerns, but she is remembered for her stunning beauty and sex appeal. Hall also starred alongside John Wayne and Tom Mix. Wayne considered Hall one of his favorite leading ladies. Pokrifcsak Collection.*

Early Westerns ended typically with the cowboy hero saving the life or ranch of the female costar. Silent movie star William S. Hart is shown here embracing Jane Novak as Ethel Barton in the seven-reel Western Three Word Brand, *1921. Gish Collection.*

"I remember doubling for a star on the Beverly Hills bridle path one day," McGinnis recalled, "and doing five falls off a cantering horse for ten bucks a fall." The job was unyielding and underpaid. "But, I was glad to get the work; my only complaint was there wasn't enough of it."

Some cowgirls did make reasonable amounts of money. Bonnie Gray, who often substituted for cowboys Bing Crosby, Hoot Gibson, and Buck Jones, earned $10,000 for jumping a horse over a pile of brush and down a ten-foot cliff. The horse landed such that the stirrup straps broke and Gray sustained a backward fall. She commented that

A pistol-packin' Bessie Barrlscale is featured here in Two Gun Betty. The costumes worn by both cowgirl and cowboy stars during the 'teens and 1920s are remarkably accurate. Period chaps, holsters, and hats were plentiful and inexpensive. These early movies reflected more accurately the real West, since many of the stars had worked on ranches or had performed in the rodeo arena. Gish Collection.

Sally Blane of Salida, Colorado and Randolph Scott starred in the 1932 Paramount Western Wild Horse Mesa. Blane made less than a dozen Westerns, but they were better than the popular "B" Westerns. During this time, film scripts relied more on plot and dialogue than on action. Glamour and acting skill became more important for cowgirl starlets than their riding ability. Rainey Collection.

In the early 1940s, Nell O'Day starred in thirteen of Johnny Mack Brown's Westerns. She performed stunts on her horse Shorty. Before becoming a Western star, she had appeared on Broadway. Subsequently, she worked as a writer and editor. Rainey Collection.

she would never do the stunt again, but few who knew her were convinced. "I used to ride to Beverly Hills and practice my stunts on Will's (Will Rogers's) front lawn," Gray said. Cowgirl Florence Randolph was hired for five minutes of stunt riding, at $200-300. One stunt in which she doubled for Shirley Mason in *Resin* and rode horses off cliffs evolved into a one-month engagement. Hollywood failed to retain her full attention: "I had the rodeo fever, so I left Hollywood and went back to Texas." Rodeo cowgirl Mildred Douglas went to Mixville, Mix's movie set, and starred in some of his films. She used to drive through Hollywood with a trained leopard in her red sports car, both presents from Mix. Although Douglas enjoyed shopping and wearing fine clothes, she soon tired of the work and returned to her first love, riding bucking broncs.

With the development of the talkies in the 1930s and 1940s, Westerns became much more predictable. Cowboys and their horses received top billing, whereas Western women lost their silent-movie status to supporting roles. In Barbara Stanwyck's

188

first Western *Annie Oakley* (1935), producers chose to downplay the character of the heroine by demeaning her marksmanship and by creating the illusion of subjugation of career for family. Stanwyck, an admirer of pioneer women, complained about this treatment of Oakley's legacy and about the plots of other Western films in which women were left behind "with the kids and the cows." Cowboy characters often exhibited hostility towards women. As Jane Tompkins wrote in her book *West Of Everything*, the Western evolved into a man's world, in which men were trying constantly to escape women, whom they equated with civilization. "The Western turned against organized religion and the whole woman's culture of the nineteenth century and all the sermons and novels that

(opposite) **Barbara Stanwyck starred in Annie Oakley in 1935. The film was the actress's first Western, for which she was obliged to learn to ride and handle a gun. Stanwyck went on to become a well-known Western star in a number of films including Union Pacific, California, Cattle Queen of Montana, and Forty Guns. In April 1973, the Hall of Fame of Great Western Performers at the National Cowboy Hall of Fame inducted Stanwyck for "Outstanding Contribution to the West through Motion Pictures." Stanwyck also starred in the television show, The Big Valley, which ran from 1965 to 1969.**

went with them." Men sought the West for their own identity. In *Tall In The Saddle* (1944), John Wayne remarked to a ranch woman, "You might as well know right now that no woman is going to get me hog tied and branded." Ironically, he does marry a woman, albeit a feisty, gun-carrying cowgirl. Women were often featured as sexual objects rather than the cowboy's equal, for example, Jane Russell in *Outlaw* (1943) and the voluptuous Jennifer Jones in *Duel In The Sun* (1946).

As the formula Western film continued to be popular, increasing numbers of women were forced to play supporting roles, an exception being Stanwyck, who portrayed the tough but feminine woman on the range in *Union Pacific* (1939) and *Cattle Queen of Montana* (1955). Dale Evans, who first appeared with Roy Rogers in the *Cowboy and the Señorita* (1944), created one of the most memorable western characters. With a generous endowment of nerve and brains, Evans was key to the plot. Young girls in the 1950s who watched the "The Roy Rogers Show" on television dreamed of growing up to be as independent and self-sufficient as Evans. She was Republic Studios' Queen of the West. Evans appeared in twenty-nine films with Rogers and received co-star billing in 1949. Gail Davis, whom Gene Autry called the perfect actress for her beauty, horsemanship, and histrionics, also inspired young girls in her successful television program, "Annie Oakley" (1953-1958). Like her namesake, this heroine was

Movie star Shirley Temple and roping celebrity Monty Montana gave a short roping performance at a Western theme party at the Desert Inn in Palm Springs, California in 1938. Montana taught Temple a few tricks that morning. Montana was one of the most famous trick-ropers of all time; his career started in 1916 and lasted seventy years. Montana Collection.

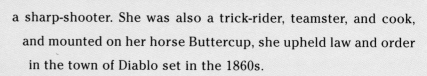

Jack Benny starred in a comedy Western entitled Buck Benny Rides Again, made by Paramount Pictures in 1940. He is surrounded here by a cavvy of stylized cowgirls.

Doris Day starred as Calamity Jane in this comedy Western for Warner Bros. in 1953.

a sharp-shooter. She was also a trick-rider, teamster, and cook, and mounted on her horse Buttercup, she upheld law and order in the town of Diablo set in the 1860s.

As women in Western films continued to play predominantly second-rate parts, cowgirls continued to work in Hollywood as stunt women. Alice Van-Springsteen doubled for such noteworthies as Dale Evans, Gail Davis in the "Annie Oakley" television series, Ingrid Bergman, Ginger Rogers, Bette Davis, Doris Day, Judy Garland, and many others. She was a trick- and fancy-rider who competed from California to Madison Square Garden. "I never lost,"she said of all her rodeo events. She rode relay horses and made flying changes quickly enough to capture the title of World Champion Cowgirl Relay Rider at Tex Austin's World Championship Cowboy Contest in Los Angeles (1933). A year earlier she performed in the opening ceremonies of the Olympic Games in Los Angeles. To augment her rodeo winnings, Van-Springsteen performed stunts in Hollywood. She drove wagons and tipped them over, jumped from buildings into hay wagons, survived bar-room fights and gunshot wounds, and in one film, jumped a horse from the edge of one cliff to another. Once Van-Springsteen was asked to jump from a cliff into a river. Minutes before the stunt she turned to the cowboy stunt man and said, "Excuse me, but I don't know how to swim. Could you make sure I don't drown?" Just as the camera man signaled from below, the cowboy answered, "I can't swim either," and they both jumped. "The producers don't train you to be a stunt person," Van-Springsteen said. "That's just up to you. You just did it. Sometimes you got hurt, but then you just go back and do it again." Early Hollywood actresses and stunt women kept the cowgirl spirit alive. They performed every conceivable feat of horsemanship and displayed professional skills coupled with their best efforts and devotion. For some of these working women, the financial rewards for their daring and athletic prowess were at least reasonable.

Bob Hope, Jane Russell, and Roy Rogers in Son of Paleface (1952). Russell, whose first film was The Outlaw (1943), attracted audiences with her sex appeal. By this time, the cowgirl star played a secondary role in Westerns. Russell's other Westerns included The Paleface (in which she portrayed Calamity Jane) (1948), Montana Belle (1952), and The Tall Men (1955).

Peggy Stewart, a "B" Western star, dresses in Hollywood cowgirl style. Hollywood's glamorous interpretation of cowgirl clothing influenced the evolution of cowgirl fashion.

Hollywood star Joan Crawford wears a fancy embroidered 1940s cowgirl outfit. These outfits had their beginnings at the turn of the century with Wild West show performers and early rodeo stars such as Prairie Rose Henderson, who wore bright colors and sequins. Commercial costume designers and manufacturers such as Nudie of Hollywood, Nathan Turk, and Hollywood Ben took the embellished western costume to its highest level during the 1940s and 1950s. Nyhom Collection.

JOAN'S GREATEST TRIUMPH

HERBERT J. YATES
presents

JOAN CRAWFORD

in

"JOHNNY GUITAR"

TRUCOLOR BY CONSOLIDATED

starring

STERLING HAYDEN · SCOTT BRADY
MERCEDES McCAMBRIDGE

with BEN COOPER · ERNEST BORGNINE · WARD BOND · JOHN CARRADINE

Screen Play by PHILIP YORDAN · Based on the novel by ROY CHANSLOR

Associate Producer-Director NICHOLAS RAY

A REPUBLIC PICTURE

In 1954, Joan Crawford played a hard-fisted, gun-totin' cowgirl in the twisted western Johnny Guitar. Pokrifcsak Collection.

Louise Currie, a Hollywood Western star, is shown in this publicity photo with a bull whip and six-shooter. By the 1940s, Westerns featured glamorous cowgirls in contrast to the tough women riders of the past. Rainey Collection.

In 1941 Gene Tierney and Randolph Scott starred in the film Belle Starr, The Bandit Queen of the West. The real Belle Starr, who was a horse thief that also sheltered outlaws, was much tougher and more exciting than the character in this "B" Western. Pokrifcsak Collection.

A cowgirl cracking a bull whip was a popular western image. Jean Arthur, whose movie career started in the 1920s, starred in Arizona (1940). Her other two memorable films included Cecil B. DeMille's The Plainsman (1936), in which she co-starred with Gary Cooper, and Shane (1953). Surprisingly, this star was plagued with stage fright throughout her successful career. Rainey Collection.

Dale Evans was the most beloved of all cowgirl film stars. She made over two dozen Westerns beginning in the 1940s with her husband Roy Rogers. She went on to star with Rogers in their popular television series and performed in over one hundred episodes that began in 1953.

Gail Davis starred in a popular television series, Annie Oakley, which aired in 1953. Davis played a young Annie, who was a crack shot and expert rider, living in a mythical town in the southwest called Diablo. The show went off the air in 1956 after eighty-one episodes.

Merchandising was an important part of selling the cowgirl image to the children of the 1950s. This fancy-fringed ensemble was licensed by Dale Evans. With this outfit and toy six-shooter, every little girl could dream of emulating her cowgirl hero. High Noon Collection.

Jane Fonda starred in the popular western comedy Cat Ballou , made in 1965. Her role as a strong independent Westerner made an unusual statement, given the secondary roles played by women in contemporary Westerns.

Alice Van-Springsteen was a real rodeo star and stunt woman. She doubled for Gail Davis in Annie Oakley and later for Dale Evans during the course of The Roy Rogers Show. Van-Springsteen is shown here doing a stunt jump across a dangerous railroad cut. Stunt riders and horses were so inexpensive that special effects were rarely used in the early Westerns. Van-Springsteen Collection.

GIRLS OF THE GOLDEN WEST

CHAPTER 6

Despite the paucity of cowgirls relative to cowboys, image makers capitalized on the opportunity to cultivate the unconventional "Girl of the Golden West". The title of a play by David Belasco in 1905 about a saloon-keeper who falls in love with an outlaw, and the title of Giacomo Puccini's opera written in 1910 (the first grand opera written on an American theme), the Girl of the Golden West became a romantic name for a spirited western heroine. As proven by Buffalo Bill's Wild West Show, the cowgirl played by Annie Oakley was an enchanting star. Especially responsive to her youth, audiences admired her ability as a lady to compete in a man's world. Some critics believe that Annie Oakley attracted more attention than the infamous Buffalo Bill.

As early as 1890, the cowgirl's image was used in advertising. Her spirit and independence attracted the male buyer to a pastiche of products including ammunition, guns, coffee, beer, cigarettes, cigars, saddles, dry goods, shoes, John Deere tractors, buggies, war bonds, and liquor. Many business entrepreneurs also used calendars featuring good-looking cowgirls.

Dime novelists, as well as magazine editors, novelists, theater directors, and song-writers, utilized the theme of women in the Golden West. These media tantalized readers with color covers of attractive women riding horses, driving stagecoaches, and "packing iron." The so-called "pulp" publications featured action with titles such as *Winchester Wedding*, *Wild Princess of Pistol Basin*, *Outcast Ladies Can't Survive*, and *Pounding Hoofs and Hearts*. During this time, the railroads issued brochures promoting the dude ranch industry. Invariably, a sporty-looking cowgirl with her pony was illustrated on the front cover. In 1935, "I Want To be a Cowgirl Sweetheart" reached number one on the Western charts,

A cowgirl from the 101 Ranch in Oklahoma packs a Colt Bisley Single Action in her holster. At the turn of the century, the image of the cowgirl riding a horse with a six-shooter on her waist was well-established. Manns Collection.

(opposite) *This calendar art from 1906 features a galloping cowgirl. Artwork of this nature showed the rest of the world that the women of the Golden West were competent equestriennes that enjoyed an independence ahead of their time. Manns Collection.*

197

HURRAH! A RACE! A RACE! THE COW-BOY GIRL WINS.

KILROY & BRITTON, PRESENT—
THE MUSICAL-MELO-DRAMA
THE COW-BOY GIRL
AND A BUNCH OF SINGERS AND DANCERS
7 BIG SONGS

No Advance in Prices

FOX
3 Days Starting, MONDAY, MAY 6
A GENUINE THEATRICAL NOVELTY A POSITIVE TREAT.
THE COW BOY GIRL
A DRAMA FILLED WITH THRILLING EPISODES DELIGHTFUL COMEDY AND BREEZY MUSIC
THE BIGGEST MELO-DRAMATIC MUSICAL FUNNY PLAY OF THE YEAR!!
GYP AND HER FRISKY BRONCO — A BEVY OF PRETTY SHOW GIRLS!!!
IN THE WAY
COMING SOON

KILROY & BRITTON'S
THE MUSICAL MELO-DRAMA

THE COW-BOY GIRL

MUSICAL SELECTIONS

THE COW-BOY GIRL	50
ALL THE WORLD'S IN LOVE	50
THERE'S NO FOOL LIKE AN OLD FOOL	50
WHITTLING DUET	50
HE TREATED ME WHITE	50
FOUR BAD MEN FROM ARIZONEY	50
BOSTON TOURIST GIRLS	50

Will Rossiter
Publisher
CHICAGO, ILL.
COPYRIGHT MCMVI BY WILL ROSSITER

and Patsy Montana thus became the first woman to sell a million copies of a country-western song. The cowgirl was clearly established in American culture.

Cowboys at the turn of the century wrote songs about her diverse personality. One ballad included in *Cowboy Songs and Frontier Ballads,* by John and Alan Lomax, praised a Miss Mollie: "She was a lovely western girl, as lovely as could be;/She was so tall, so handsome, so charming, and so fair." "My Love is a Rider," featured in Jack Thorp's *Songs of a Cowboy,* recognized a cowgirl's equestrian ability and daring:

(opposite) The musical stage play The Cow-Boy Girl opened in 1912. The term cow-boy girl was used from 1890-1912 before the term cowgirl took its place. Schmitt/Cayuse Collection.

My love is a rider, wild broncos she breaks,
Though she promised to quit it, just for my sake.

Finally, like the cowboy, cowgirls misbehaved. Thorp discovered this song about a female outlaw:

Hunted by many a posse,
Always on the run,
Every man's hand against them,
They fought, and often won.

A number of books portrayed the cowgirl as an attractive, self-reliant character. In Francis Parker's *Hope Hathaway* (1904) and Emerson Hough's *North of 36* (1923), cowgirls dominate the plot. Hope Hathaway carries a gun, apprehends outlaws, and finally captures a husband. In *North of 36,* Taisie Lockhart takes over her family's failing ranch and drives one of the first herds of cattle over the Chisholm Trail. These authors, however, were challenged by the scope of the cowgirl character. Although Lockhart initially wears pants, she dons a lavish ball gown to greet a handsome cowboy in the parlor.

Hollywood also struggled with the portrayal of the cowgirl. Originally she was the cowboy's equal, riding recklessly, swinging from trains, and capturing outlaws. In the 1930s-1940s movie producers emphasized her sex appeal over her pioneering skills.

The musical Cow-Boy Girl featured one song entitled Four Bad Men From Arizona. The title song, The Cow-Boy Girl, featured lyrics praising the cowgirl's roping and riding skills. Cervone Collection.

One critic summed up the Western heroine at this point as the "weak and defenseless female, without any personality of her own, essentially dependent on the hero," or as "the titillatingly sexual and aggressive heroine." It seemed Hollywood was equally undecided.

By 1950, marketing experts designing cowgirl images appropriated portraits from Hollywood as well as from rodeo. Dale Evans had become a star, and in the rodeo arena beautiful sponsor girls had replaced the daring athletes of the past. Calendar advertisements and a popular chocolate company featured cute cowgirls in short skirts and fringe. In campy ads for Coca-Cola, she was sweet, perky, and decidedly more sexy in comparison to earlier cowgirl images. During this time, a number of professionals complained about the distasteful use of women as sex objects in advertisements. This awareness corrected the offenses only minimally, because sexy images sold products.

In 1975, Margaret C. Formby founded The National Cowgirl Hall of Fame and Western Heritage Center in the small cowtown of Hereford, Texas. "The idea just caught my fancy and I thought the cowgirls had been undersold for too long. We uncovered a gold mine, history that nobody was keeping up with. The cowgirls performed and did what they loved to do, but they never really got their names up in lights like they should have." In 1993, the Cowgirl Hall of Fame was moved to Fort Worth, with a mission to expand and share the cowgirl story with more people. The Hall, which was subsequently named the National Cowgirl Museum and Hall of Fame, hoped to inspire others to live their lives with as much commitment and courage as evidenced by women of the American West.

Fern Sawyer, rodeo star of the 1930s and 1940s, champion cutting horse rider, and National Cowgirl Museum and Hall of Fame honoree, epitomized the old-time cowgirl's virtues. "I have a great philosophy of life," she told author Teresa Jordan in her book *Cowgirls, Women of the American West*. "Do all you can as fast as you can. If I had to do it over, I'd do the same thing, only a little more of it." In addition to her passion for ranching, she had confidence in success. "I believe you prove what you can do. If you're good enough, you'll get there. You can't tell me that in America, if you're good at your job, you won't make it. I've seen too many of them make it." Sawyer clearly had little use for the platform of the

"Cheyenne" was a popular song during the first decade of the century. Before the phonograph, pianos were the most popular form of home entertainment. Scores of songs paid tribute to the cowgirl. Schmitt/Cayuse Collection.

(opposite) Sheet music featured cowgirls as the pride of the prairie and as lady bronc riders. Lyrics conveyed romance and life on the range. Schmitt/Cayuse and Williams Collections.

" I'm strong enough to fight my own battles, and I will. . ."

Hope Hathaway

The novel Hope Hathaway by Frances Parker (1904) is one of the few novels about a strong-minded ranch woman who defends a sheepherder, whom she subsequently married. The lead character, Hope Hathaway, dresses in a split riding skirt, rides as well as a cowboy, and is handy with a gun. At the start of the book she says: "I'm strong enough to fight my own battles, and I will..." When men threaten to take over some of her father's property, Hope Hathaway defends the land. One of the final scenes takes place in a corral where Hathaway protects herself and her lover by shooting a cowboy in the wrist. Healey Collection.

202

women's liberation movement. Connie Douglas Reeves, another great Texas horsewoman and a riding coach at the well-known Waldemar Camp for Girls in Hunt, Texas, shared Sawyer's passion for living. "Of all things in nature, sunrises appeal to me most. I feel like with a new day there is great opportunity." For Reeves it was also important to be able to "saddle her own horse."

The cowgirl, although she was independent, could also be a team player. "I feel a woman should walk beside her husband, not in front of him. If you lead the way doing the work, you will find you have the pleasure of doing all of the work by yourself," wrote Linda Velder of South Dakota for the anthology *Leaning into the Wind*. In contrast, trick-rider and rancher Audrey Hodges of Salmon, Idaho discovered that her work ethic and drive always exceeded those of her respective three husbands.

Hope Hathaway is an unusual tale because the main character is a cowgirl. The book is also important because the story was illustrated by Western painter Charles M. Russell. Russell, who was known for his true-to-life portraits of cowboy life at the turn of the century, rarely painted females. His illustrations show unusual images of Hope Hathaway dressed in authentic western attire. Healey Collection.

Dime novels were popular from the late 1860s to 1920s. They were usually produced in a series featuring a single heroine. Stella was one of many cowgirl heroines. Manns Collection.

Ranch Romances was a popular pulp magazine in the 1930s. This series featured action-packed western stories about cowboys and cowgirls.

A pulp cover, c. 1935, by Fred Craft. Typically cowboys saved or protected cowgirls in these illustrations. Silva Collection.

(opposite) Western artist W. Herbert Dunton painted this cowgirl in 1908. She represents the ideal cowgirl of the period: beautiful, poised, and comfortable in the saddle. This illustration was widely used for magazine covers and calendar art. Lebel Collection.

SUNDAY MAGAZINE
Of the St. Louis Republic

ST. LOUIS, MISSOURI
FEBRUARY 7, 1909
PART 3
20 PAGES

The image of the cowgirl was used to sell a wide variety of products from candy to coffee. Advertisers believed her sweet, independent character attracted male buyers. Holley Collection.

Hyer was one of the major boot manufacturers prior to World War II. He obviously hoped to attract cowgirl shoppers with this catalog cover.

Early cigarette manufacturers tried to convince cowboys to smoke ready-made cigarettes by their portrayal of a cowgirl representing their product. Forty years later, Chesterfield also featured a cowgirl, but by that time it had become acceptable for women to smoke in public. Filler Collection.

Walk-Over Shoe Company used this sweet, pistol-packin' cowgirl to sell their line of lace-up boots, c. 1908. Lebel Collection.

207

(opposite and above) **Washington's Rainier brewing company used this charming cowgirl mounted on a stylish horse with a horsehair bridle for their 1906 calendar. A small notebook with the same image was produced as a give-away. Sheppard Collection.**

This metal beer tray features an enamel image of a cowgirl riding astride, c. 1910. Lebel Collection.

Coca-Cola used the image of the cowgirl on numerous advertising signs and in ad campaigns throughout the 1940s and 1950s. Flood Collection.

209

Calendar art was one of the most popular uses for cowgirl imagery. The artist typically portrayed cowgirls in buckskin outfits with six-shooters on their hips. Many of these images were considered scandalous in Victorian times. Holley Collection.

1926		January			1926	
SUN.	MON.	TUE.	WED.	THU.	FRI.	SAT.
					1	2
3	4	5	6	7	8	9
10	11	12	13	14	15	16
17	18	19	20	21	22	23
24/31	25	26	27	28	29	30

(above and opposite) **Calendars that hung in butcher shops and lumber companies during the first decade of the 1900s often featured a pretty cowgirl and her pony. This image appealed to many male viewers, who possibly fantasized about another life on a ranch accompanied by a cowgirl sweetheart. Lebel Collection.**

(above and opposite) *Cheesecake became popular during World War II. Advertisers recycled these provocative images of cowgirls well into the mid-1960s. Stuckey Collection.*

The image of a cowgirl with a Palomino and silver parade saddle attracted attention in the 1950s. These models, with their flashy boots and tack, reflected a showy Hollywood cowgirl style. High Noon Collection.

213

This postcard of the Cheyenne Girl, whipping and spurring her pony, sold in western stores from 1905 to 1910. Tourists sent cards home to show family and friends what cowgirls in the West were really like. Manns Collection.

The cowgirl image continues to evolve. Washington Mutual Bank in the state of Washington recently initiated an advertising campaign, "That's Different, That's Washington Mutual," to celebrate eccentric characters. Jim Walker and his colleagues at the advertising firm of McCann-Erickson in Seattle attempted to create phrases out of two apparently unrelated words. "Someone said 'rodeo grandmas' and we all laughed and wondered if they existed," Walker said. Through connections in the ranching community of Ellensburg, Washington, Walker discovered four authentic ranch and rodeo women, between the ages of fifty-seven and eighty-seven: Judy Golladay, Peggy Minor Hunt, Janis Capezzoli Anderson, and Lorraine Plass. The response to the first ad, which featured team-roping, trick-roping, barrel racing, and herding cattle in a rainstorm, was so overwhelming that the grandmas made national news. The three ads, including one in which the grandmas stop a stagecoach, were unique because the grandmas were genuine. Moreover, the cowgirl image emerged as a role model that appealed to all ages and personalities. Young adults and their parents appreciated the grandmas' unconventional style of aging, and senior citizens were proud to have their contemporaries honored. The grandmas' biggest fans, however, are their own grandchildren, who stand on the sidelines and cheer: "Go, Granny, go."

Golladay worked up until the time she died of breast cancer in 1998. Her friends joked that if she could have put headlights on her horse, she would have worked cattle all night. Hunt, a trick-roping star from the 1940s, can still jump through a loop and spends time teaching her grandchildren horsemanship skills. Anderson continues to rope with her family and to pass on her heritage of ranching, team work, and family pride. Plass, dressed in her green-fringed jacket and flat-crown, silver-belly hat, trails behind the family's cattle and cracks her bull whip. Like all the old-time cowgirls, Plass's spirit is gloriously stubborn. "As long as the colt stays under me I'll do all right. I will get the job done." As Dale Evans once said of a great cowgirl, "You're something else honey." Let 'er buck!

(left and opposite) *In a brief forty-year period, the image of the cowgirl changed from this independent Texas cowgirl with her pistol on her hip (c. 1908) to the scantily-clad cowgirl of the late 1940s, titled "Aim To Please." The degree to which the cowgirl image changed over such a short period of time is remarkable. Walden/Rattenbury Collections.*

Advertisers promoting politicians, funeral homes, and lumber companies gave away cardboard hand fans with attached wooden handles in the days before electric fans and air conditioning. Some fans were embossed or were simply printed. The advertiser's name appeared on the back. This group of fans features cowgirls on horseback and traveling with guns. DeBeer Collection.

By World War I, the cowgirl image had become an American icon for a spirited character. This photo album appeared c. 1918. DeBeer Collection.

Cowgirl postcards sold well in
western stores at the turn of the
century. Cowgirls were exotic
but socially acceptable women in
America during the first two decades
of this century. Painter Collection.

782.   Cow Puncher Girl.

4008   READY FOR THE ROUNDUP

A Daughter
of the West

Eastern dudes often had their photograph taken during visits to Cheyenne, Wyoming, or Pendleton, Oregon for one of the major rodeos. Like this woman, they enjoyed dressing for the camera; note the woolly chaps, bandana, and "hog leg," c. 1930. Schmitt/Cayuse Collection.

After seeing a Wild West show or visiting a dude ranch, many women wanted to be cowgirls. A young girl with cuffs, a small pistol, and a quirt at her feet is the subject of this elaborate studio photograph, c. 1910. Walden Collection.

(opposite) Easterners as well as Europeans fantasized about Wild West women, packing six-shooters and riding across the plains. This embossed lithograph was printed in Germany, c. 1905. High-quality prints such as this one often decorated saloon walls. Benson Collection.

Sissy is decked out in her western play suit. Many children, inspired by the horse operas of the 1930s, in which Tom Mix and Buck Jones starred with "B" actresses, dressed western and played cowboys and Indians with the boys. Manns Collection.

(above right) A young cowgirl on her pony poses for a photographer. Many of these little girls realized their dreams by joining the rodeo in later years. Note her spotted bridle and fancy heart breast collar. Photograph, c. 1935. Harman Collection.

The little girls who grew up still wanting to be cowgirls continued to have their photographs taken in buckaroo duds, c. 1940. Schmitt/Cayuse Collection.

(opposite) The rodeo grandmas (left to right) Peggy Minor Hunt, Lorraine Plass, Janis Capezzoli Anderson, and Judy Golladay dressed in vintage attire for a Washington Mutual advertising campaign, created by McCann-Erickson in Seattle, Washington in 1997. The grandmas, their feisty spirit and old-time look, attracted so much attention that they ended up on the Rosie O'Donnell show and as celebrities in local parades. The grandmas proved that the cowgirl has become an enduring image of American independence. Dale Windham photo.

BIBLIOGRAPHY

Ahlborn, Richard E. *Man Made Mobile, Early Saddles of Western North America*. Washington D.C.: Smithsonian Institution Press, 1980.

Beach, Cora A. *Women of Wyoming*. Casper, Wyoming: S.E. Boyer & Co., 1927.

Beauchamp, Carl. *Without Lying Down, Frances Marion and the Powerful Women of Early Hollywood*. New York: A Lisa Drew Book, Scribner, 1997.

Bird, Isabella L. Bird. *A Lady's Life in the Rocky Mountains*. Norman and London: University of Oklahoma Press, 1960.

Bird, Sarah. *Virgin of The Rodeo*. New York: Bantam Books, 1993.

Blankenship, Mary A. *The West Is For Us, The Reminiscences of Mary A. Blankenship*. Lubbock: West Texas Museum Association, 1953.

Borne, Lawrence R. *Dude Ranching, A Complete History*. Albuquerque: University of New Mexico Press, 1983.

Bourne, Eulalia. *Woman in Levi's*. Flagstaff: University of Arizona Press, 1967.

Brown, Dee. *The Gentle Tamers: Women of the Old Wild West*. Lincoln: University of Nebraska Press, 1981 [1958].

Brownlow, Kevin & John Kobal. *Hollywood, The Pioneers*. New York: Alfred A. Knopf, 1979.

Burns, Mamie Sypert. *This I Can Leave You, A Woman's Day On The Pitchfork Ranch*. Texas: A & M University Press, 1986.

Burt, Nathaniel. *Jackson Hole Journal*. Norman: University of Oklahoma Press, 1983.

Burt, Struthers. *The Diary of a Dude-Wrangler*. New York: Charles Scribner's Sons, 1924.

Clancy, Foghorn. *My Fifty Years in Rodeo: Living With Cowboys, Horses and Danger*. San Antonio: Naylor, 1952.

Cleavland, Agnes Morley. *No Life For a Lady*. Lincoln: University of Nebraska Press, 1977 [1941].

Collings, Ellsworth, and Alma Miller England. *The 101 Ranch*. Norman: University of Oklahoma Press, 1938.

Conrad, Barnaby III. *Ghost Hunting in Montana, A Search for Roots in the Old West*. New York: Harpers CollinsWest, 1994.

Crandall, Judy. *Cowgirls: Early Images and Collectibles*. Atglen, Penn.: Schiffer Publishing Ltd, 1994.

Fenin George N., and William K. Everson. *The Western: From Silents to the Seventies*. New York: Grassman, 1973.

Flood, Elizabeth Clair. *Dude Ranches Out West*. Salt Lake City: Gibbs Smith, Publisher, 1995.

Flynn, Shirley E. Flynn. *Let's Go! Let's Show! Let's Rodeo!, The History of Cheyenne Frontier Days*. Cheyenne: Wigwam Publishing Company, LLC 1996.

Hasselstrom, Linda, Gaydell Collier, and Nancy Curtis. *Leaning Into the Wind*. Boston, New York: Houghton Mifflin Company, 1997.

Havighurst, Walter. *Annie Oakley of the Wild West*. Lincoln: University of Nebraska Press, 1954.

Hough, Emerson. *North of 36*. New York: Grosset & Dunlap Publishers, 1923.

Hough, Donald. *The Cocktail Hour in Jackson Hole*. Wyoming: High Plains Publishing Company, 1951.

Hufsmith, George W. *The Lynching of Cattle Kate 1889*. Glendo, Wyo.: High Plains Press, 1993.

Hunter, Marvin J. *The Trail Drivers of Texas*. Austin: University of Texas Press, 1924.

Jordan, Teresa. *Cowgirls: Women of the American West*. Lincoln: University of Nebraska Press, 1992.

King, Bucky. *The Dude Connection*. Sheridan: Jelm Mountain Press, 1983.

LeCompte, Mary Lou. *Cowgirls of The Rodeo: Pioneer Professional Athletes*. Urbana: University of Illinois Press, 1993.

Leffingwell, Mary. *Diamonds in the Snow*. Big Timber, 1992.

Larson, Helen Kay Brander. *Brander Sisters Let 'er Buck*. 1975.

Lomax, John and Alan. *Cowboy Songs and Other Frontier Ballads*. New York: Macmillan, 1938.

Lucey, Donna M. *Photographing Montana 1894-1928: The Life and Work of Evelyn Cameron*. New York: Alfred A. Knopf, 1991.

Luchetti, Cathy. *"I Do" Courtship, Love and Marriage on the American Frontier, A Glimpse at America's Romantic Past Through Photographs, Diaries and Journals 1715-1915*. New York: Crown Trade Paperbacks, 1996.

Martin, Ralph G. *The Extraordinary Life of Eleanor Medill Patterson*. New York: Simon & Schuster, 1979.

McEwen, Christian. *Jo's Girls, Tomboy Tales of High Adventure, True Grit, and Real Life*. Boston: Beacon Press, 1997.

McGinnis, Vera. *Rodeo Road, My Life As A Pioneer Cowgirl*. New York: Hastings, 1974.

Moore, Louis C. *The Imposters of Monterey, Bouchard and One-Eyed Charley*. Monterey, California: Angel Press/Publishers, 1985.

The Oxford History of World Cinema. Edited by Geoffrey Nowell-Smith. Oxford, New York: Oxford University Press, 1996.

Parker, Frances. *Hope Hathaway*. Boston: CM Clark Publishing Company, 1904.

Peavy, Linda & Ursala Smith. *Pioneer Women, The Lives of Women On The Frontier*. New York: Smithmark, 1996.

Rainey, Buck. *Sweethearts of the Sage, Biographies and Filographies of 258 Actresses Appearing in Western Movies*. Jefferson, North Carolina and London: McFarland & Company, Inc. Publishers, 1992.

Ryan, Kathleen Jo, *Ranching*. New York: Abbeville Press, 1989.

Reeves, Constance Douglas. *I Married a Cowboy*. Austin: Eakin Press, 1995.

Reiter, Joan Swallow. *The Women*. New York: Time-Life Books, 1978.

Riske, Milt. *Those Magnificent Cowgirls: A History of the Rodeo Cowgirl*. Cheyenne: Wyoming Publishing, 1983.

Roach, Joyce Gibson. *The Cowgirls*. Texas: University of North Texas Press, 1990 [1977].

Rogers, Roy, and Dale Evans with Michale and Jane Stern. *Happy Trails: Our Life Story*. New York: Simon and Schuster, 1994.

Savage, Candace. *Cowgirls*. Berkeley, California: Ten Speed Press, 1996.

Shawver, Mary. *Sincerely Mary S*. Casper, Wyoming: Prairie Publishing Company.

Schlissel, Lillian, Vicki L. Ruiz, and Janice Monk, eds. *Western Women: Their Land, Their Lives.* Albuquerque: University of New Mexico Press, 1988.

Shirley, Glen. *Belle Starr and Her Times, The Literature, the Facts, and the Legends.* Norman: University of Oklahoma Press, 1982.

Smith, Lawrence B. *Dude Ranches and Ponies.* New York: Coward-McCann, 1936.

Sollid, Roberta Beed. *Calamity Jane: A Study in Historical Criticism.* Helena, Mont.: Western Press, 1958

Stansbury, Kathryn B. *Lucille Mulhall, Wild West Cowgirl.* Mulhall, Oklahoma: Homestead Heirlooms Publishing Company, 1985.

Stern, Jane & Michael. *Way Out West.* New York: HarperCollins, 1993.

Stewart, Elinore Pruitt. *Letters of a Woman Homesteader.* Lincoln: University of Nebraska Press, 1961.

Stillwell, Hallie Crawford. *I'll Gather My Geese.* Texas: Texas A & M University Press, 1991 [1914]·

Tanner, Ogden. *The Ranchers.* Alexandria, Virginia: Time-Life Books, 1977.

Thompson, Peggy & Usukawa Saeko. *Tall In The Saddle, Great Lines From Classic Westerns.* San Francisco: Chronicle Books, 1998.

Thorp, N. Howard. *Songs of the Cowboys.* New York: Clarkson N. Potter, 1960.

Tompkins, Jane. *West of Everything, The Inner Life of Westerns.* New York, Oxford: Oxford University Press, 1992.

VanCleve, Spike. *40 Years' Gatherin's.* Kansas City: The Lowell Press, 1988.

Vernam, Glenn R. *Man on Horseback.* New York: Harper & Row Publishers, Inc., 1964.

Wlaschin, Ken. *The Illustrated Encyclopedia of The World's Great Movie Stars and Their Films-From 1900 to Present Day.* New York: Bonanza Books, 1979.

Wheelwright, Jane Hollister. *The Ranch Papers, a California Memoir.* Santa Monica: The Lapis Press, 1988.

Wilbur-Cruce, Eva Antonia. *A Beautiful, Cruel Country.* Arizona, The University of Arizona Press, 1987.

Wills, Kathy Lynn, and Virginia Artho. *Cowgirl Legends from the Cowgirl Hall of Fame.* Layton, Utah: Gibbs-Smith, 1995.

Wister, Owen. *The Virginian.* New York: The Macmillan Company, 1902.

Woerner, Gail. *Belly Full of Bedsprings, The History of Bronc Riding.* Austin, Texas: Eakin Press, 1998.

Wood-Clark, Sarah. *Beautiful Daring Western Girls: Women of the Wild West Shows.* Cody, Wyo.: Buffalo Bill Historical Center, 1991 [1985].

PERIODICALS

Allen, Michael. "Mabel Strickland, Rodeo Cowgirl," *The Ketch Pen*, December-January, 1993-1994.

Cameron, Evelyn J. "The Cowgirl in Montana," *Country Life*, June 6, 1914.

Clark, Helen. "Grand Old Lady of Rodeo," *Western Horseman*, September 1959.

Fredriksson, Kristine. "Growing Up on the Road: The Children of Wild West Shows and Rodeo," *Journal of American Culture*, Fall, 1985.

Greenough, Alice. "Cowgirls of Yesterday," *Persimmon Hill*, Vol. 3.

Holt, R.D. "Side Saddle Riding," *The Cattleman*, 1956.

Jordan, Teresea. "Cowgirls, How The Fairer Sex Succeeded In the Rough World of Rodeo," *True West*, July 1983.

King, Evelyn. "Cattle Queens of the West," *Persimmon Hill*, Vol. 14, 1986.

Livingston, Donna. "Cowgirls of the Wild West," *Glenow Magazine*, July-August 1985.

Marvin, Dee. "Fannie Sperry Wowed 'Em At First Calgary Stampede," *American West*, August 1987.

Matteson, Jeanne. "Cowgirls in the Chutes," *The Lariat*, November 1990.

Porter, Willard H. "When they Took the West to London," *True West*, September 1985.

Propst, Nell Brown. "A Foot In Each World," *True West*, June 1979.

Rattenbury, Richard. "A Century of Western Fashion," *Persimmon Hill*, Autumn 1989.

Steele, Fanny Sperry as told to Helen Clark. "A Horse Beneath Me… Sometimes," *True West*, January-February 1976.

Stiffler, Liz and Tona Blake. "Fanny Sperry-Steele: Montana's Champion Bronc Rider," *Montana: The Magazine of Western History*, Spring 1982.

Taillon, C.Y. "The Preening of the Western Bird," *Western Horseman*, September 1958.

__. "Tad Lucas: World Champion," *Western Horseman*, April 1965.

__. "World Famous Cowgirl: Gene Krieg Creed," *The Ketch Pen*, 1986.

Winther, Oscar Osburn. "California Stage Company in Oregon," *Oregon Historical Society Quarterly*, 1934.

NEWSPAPERS

Denver Rocky Mountain News. "Cowboy Jo Was a Woman," March 13, 1904.

Denver Rocky Mountain News. "The Reigning Modes," December 15, 1889.

Great Falls Tribune. "Women's Ex-Rodeo Champ Still Active at 67," January, 9 1955.

The Independent Record. "Fanny Sperry Steele Lives Alone With Her Memories," December 10, 1961.

The Sunday Oregonian, Sunday Magazine Feature Section. "The Real Cowgirl of Ranch And Circus Ring," September 1913.

Tucson Citizen. " Sister Bourne: 'If I live again I want to teach,'" May 12, 1984.

INTERVIEWS

Burson, Polly. Interview with author. California, 1997
Van-Springsteen, Alice. Interview with the author. San Diego, California, 1997.
Rodeo Grandmas: Rodeo Grandmas Janis Capezzoli Anderson, Peggy Minor Hunt, Lorraine Plass, Judy Golladay and Chloe Weidenbach, Telephone interview, 1999.
Riley, Mitzi. Interview with author. Fort Worth, Texas, 1997.
Williams, Corinne. Interview with author. California, 1997.
Dellagana, Dorothy. Interview with author. Napa, California, 1998.
Merritt, DeDe. Interview with author. Cheyenne, Wyoming. 1997.
Renner, Alice. Telephone interview. 1998.
Thurman, Sammy. Interview with author. California, 1997.

FILMS

Loeser, Doris, prod. *"I'll Ride That Horse!"* Montana Women Bronc Riders. 27 min. KUSM/Montana Public Television and KBUY/Provo and Salt Lake, Utah, 1994. Videocassette.

Hodges, Audrey, home video, c 1930.

LETTERS

A letter to Prof. J A Hill from Charles Goodnight, 27 November, 1926. orig with Sheffy Papers-Research Center.

INDEX

GAYLORD R